ABSTRACTS OF
WILLS, INVENTORIES,
AND ADMINISTRATION
ACCOUNTS OF
LOUDOUN COUNTY, VIRGINIA
1757-1800

With Miscellaneous Data

J. ESTELLE STEWART KING

Pg. 48 Wm. Powell
Pg. 48 Thomas Green

An Improved Edition

With a New Index by
Elizabeth Petty Bentley

D0968032

Baltimore
GENEALOGICAL PUBLISHING CO., INC.
1979

PUBLISHER'S NOTE

For this improved edition the text has been re-organized
and re-typed. The entire work has been re-paged and a
table of contents and a new index added.

TABLE OF CONTENTS

NOTE

In the wills, the first date given is the date of the instrument, the second date, that of probate.

Few abbreviations have been used, and these are obvious: Wit. - Witness, Exr. - Executor and Executrix, Apprs. - Appraisers, Admr. - Administrator.

Stafford Co. , Va. was divided in 1730, and the County of Prince William was formed. In 1742, Prince William was divided, and the County of Fairfax created and named in honor of its titled proprietor.

In 1757, Fairfax County was divided and the territory west of its altered boundary christened Loudoun County.

Loudoun County was named in honor of Lord Loudoun, a representative peer of Scotland, who the year before its establishment, and during the French and Indian War, had been appointed Captain-general and Governor-in-chief of the province of Virginia, and Commander-in-chief of the British military forces in the colonies.

THOMAS, Evan
17 Sept. 1757. 6 Nov. 1757.
Legatees: David Thomas, James Thomas (sons), Jonas Potts (son-in-law),
John Langley, Benjamin Burson. Exrs: Jonas Potts. (p. 1)

DAVIS, Thomas
Probated 6 April 1758.
A nuncupative will proved by oath of Margaret Davis, mother of Thomas Da-
vis, who declared he wanted his brother John to have his possessions.

ADAMS, Elizabeth
9 May 1758. Inventory.
Administrator, Abraham Adams. Account, February Court, 1759.

POULTNEY, John
10th Day of 3rd Month, 1759. 10 April 1759.
Wife: Eleanor Poultney. Children: Anthony, Sarah and Mary. Exrs: wife,
Isaac Hollingsworth (friend) and John Hough. Wit: Mathew Linn, James
Steere, John Potter and James Steere.

DAVIS, Sarah
10 March 1759. May Court, 1759.
"Sojourner in Loudoun County." Legatees: John Davis (brother); Mary Wright
(sister); Elizabeth Thomas, Sarah Plackney (or Hackney) - niece. Exr: Rachel Davis. Wit: Thomas Kelley, William Onsley, Jonathan Davis. (p. 15)

MARCY, Charles.
12 June 1759. Inventory.
Appraisers: John Simmons, Richard Valandighan, Henry Brewer.

LINTON, Edward
13 Nov. 1759. Inventory.
Appraisers: Benjamin Grayson, Nathaniel Grigsby and Francis Paget. (p. 20)

HOLLINGSWORTH, Isaac
5th Day of 10th Month, 1759. 13 Nov. 1759.
Wife: Rachel Hollingsworth. Children: Ann, Jonah, Lydia, Phebe and unborn
child. Exrs: wife Rachel and friend John Hough. Wit: Abel Janney, John
Poultney, Edward Norton and Joseph Janney. (p. 21)

BOOTH, Robert
21 Sept. 32nd Year of the Reign of our Soverign Lord King George.
Legatees: John and James Booth (sons); daughter Jane Stump (husband Thomas
Stump); daughter Ann Chambers (hus. William); granddaughter Elizabeth
Stump; granddau. Veallator Chambers (dau. of William Chambers); William
Chambers; James Booth. Exrs: James Booth and William Chambers. Wit:
William McCoy, Henry Jackson and Alexis Jackson. (p. 24)

JENNEY, Mary
9 March 1760. 13 May 1760.
Mentions late husbands - "To be buried by side of either." Daughters: Sarah
Sinkloe, Margaret Donohow, Mary Foutch, Jean McDowell, Ann McDowell
and Rebecca Jenney. Exrs: daughters Jean McDowell and Ann McDowell.
Wit: John McCarty, Elizabeth Davis and Aneas Campbell. (p. 26)

JENKINS, Samuel
March 1760. Inventory.
Appraisers: James Coleman, Thomas Guthry, Henry Brewer. (p. 28)

SPURR, James
10 Oct. 1759. August Court, 1760.
Wife Judath Spurr. Children: Richard and Judath Spurr. Exrs: wife Judath

and son Richard Spurr. Wit: John Owen, Original William, William Hancock. (p. 29)

BLANDS, Robert
    August, 1760. Inventory.
    Appraisers: Vincent Lewis, John Lewis, Benjamin Mason. Last appraisal 11 Nov. 1760.

ADAMS, Gabriel
    30 March 1761. June Court 1761.
    Wife: Elizabeth Adams. Sons: three, but only one named, Philip Adams. Sons to stay on plantation and to be bound to my brother, William Adams, until of age of twenty-one. Exrs: brother William Adams. Wit: William Stark, William Littleton and Benoni Dement. (p. 35)

MEGEAH, Joseph
    12 March 1761. June Court, 1761.
    Wife: Mary Megeagh. Children: Thomas, Jane, Elizabeth, Jonathan, Anne and unborn child. Wit: John McItheney (McIllaheny), Joseph Yates, Philip Lynham. Extrx: wife. (p. 36)

INSLEE, Henry
    19 March 1761. 9 June 1761.
    Wife: Mary Inslee. Son: William Inslee. Jean Baly (or Baty) sister of wife; Jesse Foster. Extrx: wife. Wit: William Mead, Jacob Wildman, William Ross. (p. 37)

RADCLIFFE, John
    12 June 1761. Account of Administration
    Admtrx: Susan Radcliffe. (p. 39)

ANSLEY, Henry
    June 1761. Inventory. July 1761.
    Appraisers: Michael Minn, William Ross, Benjamin Edwards. (p. 40)

YATES, Joseph
    29th Day of 8th Month, 1761. November Court, 1761.
    Wife: Alice Yates. Sons: Robert, Benjamin, Isaac, Joseph and William Yates. Daughters: Alice, Jane, Hannah, children of daughter Providence. Exrs: wife and Israel Thompson. Wit: Francis Hague (Hogue), Thomas Lamb, William Wildman. (Quakers) (p. 44)

McGEACH, Joseph
    19 March 1762. Inventory.
    Apprs: George Gregg, Joseph Caldwell, William Gossitt. (p. 46)

ADAMS, Gabriel
    11th Day of 3rd Month, 1762. Inventory.
    Appraisers: William Stark, Richard Coleman, William Littleton.

TRAVERSE, George
    11 May 1762. Inventory.
    Appraisers: William Mosgrove, Thomas Shore, William Smith.

ROBERTS, Richard
    24 April 1762. 8 June 1762.
    Wife: Ann Roberts. Sons: Joseph, Richard, John, William Roberts. Daughters: Mary, Susanah, Ruth Green and Ann. Exrs: William Jones (friend). Wit: Lee Massey and James Steere. (p. 56)

READ, Joseph
    24 Nov. 1761. 3 July 1762.
    Wife: Barbara Read. Sons: Joseph, William and Thaddeus Read (sons of former wife), John and Reuben Read. Son Andrew Read to have land my father left me in Westmoreland Co., Va. Daughters: Elizabeth, Frances, Lettice,

Ann Read. Mother: Ruth Read. Exrs: wife and Jeremiah Hutchison. Wit: Edward Porter, Jeffrey Johnson, Mary Porter. (p. 57)

SINCKLER, Wayman
12 April 1762. 13 July 1762.
All land in Prince William Co., Va. to be divided among following named children: Alexander, Isaac, Robert, Mary, George, Wayman, Elizabeth. Wife: Hester Sinckler. Exrs: wife and Bridger Haynie (friend). Wit: Russell Wilson, George Jordan, Ann Jordan. (p. 59)

WEST, William
15 Nov. 1762. April Court, 1762.
Sons: Cato and Charles West. Exrs: Charles West and Craven Peyton. Wit: West John Hall and William Atterbury. (p. 73)

SHRIEVE, William
13 April 1758. 3 April 1763.
Legatees: Elizabeth Hulls, Mary Shrieve (sisters), James Shrieve and Benjamin Shrieve (brothers). Furniture in possession of Cornelius Clauson of Pascatuway, New Jersey, to be divided between three daughters, Sarah, Elizabeth and Mary. Son: David Shrieve. Wife: Catherine Shrieve. Exrs: wife and Anthony Russell. Wit: William Holme and Jacob Wildman. (p. 76)

SEWARD, Nicholas
3 Sept. 1762. April 1763.
Wife Ann to have entire estate, also named as executrix. Thomas Sorrell (father-in-law) and James Hamilton, Gentleman, to act as trustees of said will. Wit: Sturman Chilton, Elizabeth Chilton, Martha Sorrell. (p. 78)

OMEHUNDRO, Ann
2 Sept. 1752. 13 Sept. 1763.
All estate to son William Remey, also named as executor. Wit: Philip Headen, Elizabeth Grove and William Grove.

CHAMPE, John
30 July 1763. 8 Nov. 1763.
Son: Thomas Champe. Grandson: John Champe. Daughters: Elizabeth Jones, Susy and Ann Champe. Exrs: sons John and Thomas Champe. Wit: Thomas Hogan and George Leech.

COLEMAN, Richard
5 Oct. 1763. February Court 1764.
Wife: Eleanor Coleman. At decease of wife estate to be divided among children - James Coleman, Elizabeth Brewer, Mary Masterson and Jemimah Hurst. Exrs: wife and son James. Wit: Griffin Evans, John Gess, Elizabeth Gotcley. (p. 99)

HARRIS, Samuel
4 Jan. 1757. 14 March, 1764.
Children: David, Joseph, Samuel, William, Ann Harris. Wit: William West, Jr., Ann West and Elender Gardner. (p. 103)

REDMOND, Andrew
10 March 1764. 8 May 1764.
Son William Redmond to receive one shilling. Children: Ann, Margaret, Elizabeth, John, Sarah, and Andrew. Sons John and Andrew to be bound to Edmund Phillips (son-in-law) until twenty-one years of age. Exrs: daughter Elizabeth and Edmond Philips. Wit: Israel Thompson, Thomas Arnet. (p. 111)

SANTECLARES, Margaret (Saintclare)
17 May 1764. 11 Sept. 1764.
Daughters, Elizabeth Hampton, Rebecca Morris (granddaughter), Mary Richardson. Grandchildren: Benjamin Morris, John Hawling (?), Samuel Morris. Margaret Sainclare (granddaughter), Ann Nines (or Vines), friend. Exr: son John Santeclares. Wit: William Luckett, Charity Luckett, William Luckett,

3

Jr. (p. 115)

VANDIVER, George
16 Aug. 1764. 9 Oct. 1764.
Wife: Ann Vandiver. Children: Edward, Sarah, Tabitha and Amenthia. Exrs: William Smith, John Tyler. Wit: John Field, John Spencer, James Hall.

LONG, Thomas
7 Oct. 1764. 11 March 1765.
Late of Harford Co., New England. Estate to friend James Long (Loudoun Co.) Exr: James Long. (p. 122)

STROWD, Samuel
6th Day of 4th Month, 1765. 13 May 1765.
Wife: Ann Strowd. Daughters: Martha Pitts, Mary Potts, Phebe Beeson, Ann and Susan Strowd. Son: Samuel. George Redmand alias Strowd, son of wife. Exrs: Jonas Potts (son-in-law), James Strowd, Samuel Potts. Wit: Thomas Hatfield, Ezekiel Pitts and William Dillon. (p. 124)

WILCOXEN, John (alias Winser)
2 May 1765. June Court, 1765.
Mother: Agnes Wilcoxen. Daughter Elizabeth. Stepson: John Wilcoxen Howling (or Hawling). Exrs: wife Mary Wilcoxen and friend William Luckett, Sr. Wit: Mary Cole, William Luckett, Jr., John Hamby. (p. 125)

McGREWS, Charles
22 Dec. 1764. 29 Jan. 1765.
"Charles McGrew of Virginia, but now a sojourner in Pennsylvania, weak of body." Sons: James, John, Charles and Robert McGrews. Daughter: Elizabeth. Exrs: sons James and John McGrew. (This will was written and probated in Pa., a copy recorded in Loudoun Co.) (p. 135)

ETHEL, John
17 March 1766. May Court 1766.
All estate to wife Winnifred Ethel who is named as executrix. Wit: Thomas Lewis, Gilbert Simpson, Ferdinand O'Neal. (p. 137)

DYEL, William
21 Nov. 1765. 12 May 1766.
Wife: Elizabeth Dyel. Sons: James and Leonard Dyel. Daughters: Ann Dyer (husband James Dyer), Tibitha Dyel. Other children: William, George, Josias (?), Rebecca, Litter, Stacy and Sarah Dyel. Exrs: Joseph Stephens, William Sother. Wit: Larance Sothard, Charles G. Griffith, Sarah Sotherd. (p. 138)

GRIMES, Nicholas, Sr.
5 Aug. 1765. June Court, 1766.
Of Cameron Parish. Sons: Nicholas, Philip, Edward. Grandson: William Grimes (eldest son of William Grimes). Wit: James Donaldson, Silvester Lay, Sanford Payne. (p. 144)

HOPEWELL, John
21 March 1766. June Court, 1766.
All estate to wife and children (not named). Exrs: brother Thomas Hopewell, wife Hannah (daughter of John King). Wit: Osborn King, John King and James Donaldson. (p. 146)

WIGINGTON, James
7 Aug. 1766. 12 Aug. 1766.
Mother: Sarah Wigington. Wife: Sarah Wigington. Children mentioned but not named. All estate to be in hands of mother, should she die then in care of father-in-law, Seth Botts, mother-in-law Sebacah Botts and brother-in-law Aaron Botts. Eldest son: Benjamin Wigington. Brother John Wigington. (p. 148)

ELLIS, Robert
    26 Aug. 1766. 13 Oct. 1766.
    Wife: Mary Ellis. Sons: Jesse, Robert and Samuel Ellis. Daughters: Ruth, Nancy, Margaret and Mary (youngest). Exrs: wife, son Elias, Edward Hews. Wit: William Jones, Thomas George, Abraham Dehaven. (p. 153)

PHILLIPS, Thomas, Sr.
    11 Oct. 1766. 15 Oct. 1766.
    Legatees: brother Jenkins Phillips, sons Jenkins and Thomas Phillips, also Named as executors. Sons Millford and John Phillips. Wife: Jeanna Phillips. Daughter: Catherine Phillips. Wit: Jonas Potts, Thomas Phillips, Mary Phillips. (p. 155)

HAGUE, John
    19 April 1767. 10 Aug. 1767.
    Wife: Ann Hague. Sons: Francis, Samuel, Jonah Hague. Exrs: wife, William Mead, Sr., William Mead, Jr. Wit: Isaac Hague, Moses Rhodes, William Baker. (p. 167)

JANNEY, Mary
    26th Day of 2nd Month, 1767. August Court, 1767.
    Legatees: Mahlon Janney (only son). Daughters: Hannah Brooks (hus. James), Ruth and Mary Janney - to have all household and personal estate. Exrs: friend and kinsman John Hough and daughters Ruth and Mary. Wit: Francis Hague, Joseph Hague, Samuel Janney. (p. 169)

JACKSON, Lovell
    13 Jan. 1752. 8 June 1767.
    Of Fairfax Co. Legatees: William Bell, late of New Castle and his mother Elizabeth and Ann Batts (sister of Elizabeth Bell), all of New Castle, in Great Britain. Exrs: William Bell and his mother. Wit: W. West, John Ethell, Winnifred Ethell.

MIDDLETON, Jane
    6 Aug. 1767. 14 Sept. 1767.
    Daughters: Lettice and Hannah Middleton. Molly Middleton Brown, infant daughter of Joseph Brown. Exr: Joseph Brown. Wit: James Lane, John Miller, James Hamrick.

JOHN, James
    19 April 1767. 15 Sept. 1767.
    Wife: Mary John. Mary, dau. of wife. Wit: James Lane, John Miller, J. Hamrick.

EVANS, John
    4 Oct. 1766. November Court, 1767.
    Blacksmith. Wife: Elizabeth Evans. Sons: Griffith, William, Richard, David and Joshua. Daughters: Mary Evans, Amy Thomas and her children, Elizabeth Evans. Wit: Joseph Marshall, Nathan Davis, John Davis.

JOHN, Mary
    8 Sept. 1767. 9 Nov. 1767.
    All estate to daughter Mary and her husband Thomas Phillips. Wit: Jenkind Phillips, Conrod Shoulders and Jonas Potts. (p. 182)

MOSS, John
    29 Nov. 1761. April Court, 1768.
    Wife: Frances Moss. Daughters: Anna Talbut (to receive ten pounds curr.) Mary Lewis, Hannah Moss, Frances Moss, Elizabeth Moss. Sons: John, William and Thomas Moss. Exrs: wife and sons John, Jr. and William Moss. Wit: John Andrew, Thomas Lewis and John Fields. (p. 190)

POTTS, David
    25th Day of 4th Month, 1768. 25 May 1768.
    Wife: Ann Potts. Sons: Jonas, Samuel, David, Jonathan (to have plantation

where I now live). Daughters: Mary Bagus, Rachel Potts, Susannah Potts. Exrs: sons Samuel and David Potts. Wit: William Dillon, Thomas Lewellin, David Jenkin. (p. 194)

POTTS, Jonas
31 July 1768. 12 Sept. 1768.
Wife: Mary Potts. Sons: David, Samuel, Edward. Daughters: Hannah and Elizabeth. Mentions "all my children", brother Jonathan Potts and father David Potts (late deceased). Exrs: John Vistel, Samuel Person (brothers-in-law), of Frederick Co., Va. Wit: Samuel Potts, James Conrad, Owen Roberts. (p. 202)

SCATTERDAY, George
6 July 1768. 14 Nov. 1768.
Son: John Scatterday. Wife: Esther, to receive one-third of personal estate. Exrs: wife, friend John Crory. Wit: George Dennington, Israel Thompson, George Nixon. (p. 206)

McGEACH, Thomas
7 Nov. 1768. 13 March 1769.
Sisters: Jane, Elizabeth and Ann. Brothers: Joseph, John, William and James McGeach. Exrs: William Cravens (father-in-law), George Grigg (friend). Wit: Isaac Samuel, Owen Roberts. (p. 208)

MILLER, John
13 April 1769. 8 May 1769.
"Sick and low in condition." All estate to wife Catherine Miller. Exrs: wife and Rev. Amos Thompson. Wit: Amos Thompson, Neil Patterson and John Kevens. (p. 213)

TYLER, Ann
10 April 1769. 13 June 1769.
Ann Tyler, widow. Daughters: Susannah, Ann Tyler. Sons: John, Charles, Benjamin, William and Spence Tyler. Exrs: George West, John Peake, William Smith. Wit: William Whitely, John Taylor, William Moore. (p. 215)

MONROW, George
7 Dec. 1776. 13 June 1769.
Wife Fillis to have one-third of estate. Children: Rosannah and Sarah Monrow (or Monroe). Rev. Thompson to have care of daughters in case of death of wife. Exrs: Rev. Thompson and James Buckley. Wit: Stephen Rozel, James Buckley and Joshua Duncan. (p. 218)

JOHN, Thomas
13 July 1769. Sept. Court, 1769.
Wife: Martha John. Daughters: Mary, Sarah, Hannah and Dinah. John, Thomas and Daniel John. Exrs: Joseph Thomas and Thomas George. Wit: Allen Robinett and George Lewis. (p. 220)

BURSON, Benjamin
19 Sept. 1769. October Court, 1769.
Mention made of two sons, not named. Father, Joseph Burson, to be maintained with food and raiment fitting for a man of his age and circumstances. Exrs: wife Ann with her father, Owen Roberts. (p. 222)

MOBLEY, Samuel
16 Sept. 1769. 21 Sept. 1769.
Nuncupative will. Wife: Mary Mobley. To daughter Susannah Fauch, a negro and land in Maryland. Daughter: Mary Awbery. Jacob Fauch and wife Ann and Ann Jacobs were witnesses.

SANDERS, Philip
14 June 1769. 10 Oct. 1769.
Wife: Elizabeth Sanders. Estate to be divided between children, not named. Exrs: sons William and Benjamin. Wit: John Lewis, John Taylor. (p. 225)

WEST, William
    26 June 1769. 13 Nov. 1769.
    Sons: Charles, John, Thomas West. Grandsons: Cato and Charles West.
    Granddaughter Elizabeth West, dau. of Charles West and wife Ann. Daughter
    Ann Peyton. Grandchildren: William Peyton, Francis Peyton, Margaret Pey-
    ton, Craven Peyton, Elizabeth West (dau. of Charles West). Wife: Mary
    West. Exrs: wife, Craven Peyton, Charles West. Wit: John Hall, Betsy Hall,
    Robert Hamilton, William Baker. (p. 226)

RHODES, Moses
    July 1769. 13 Nov. 1769.
    "Very sick." Wife: Mary Rhodes. Sons: William, John and Thomas Rhodes.
    Daughters: Hannah, Mary, Abigail, Elizabeth and Ann. Exr: wife. Wit: Wil-
    liam Baker. (p. 229)

ROBERTSON, Henry
    14 Oct. 1769. 15 Nov. 1769.
    Legatee: Thomas Mattox Barrett. Extrx: wife Jenny Robertson. Wit: James
    Jenning, John Linton, Peter Carter. (p. 236)

MORIN, Joseph
    14 Nov. 1769. March 1770.
    Wife Molly to have all estate during widowhood. Sons: James, Daniel, John,
    and Joseph Morin. Daughters: Peggy, Katy, Nancy and Prudence. Exrs: John
    Metcalf, William Pickett to be overseers of will. Daughter Peggy to have
    horse, cow and calf with consent of her mother and uncle John Metcalf. (p. 237)

ARNET, Alexander
    25 Dec. 1769. March Court, 1770.
    Wife Ruth to have entire estate. Exrs: wife and son Samuel Arnet. Wit: Tho-
    mas Phillips, Margaret Boulton, David Boulton.

ANDREWS, John
    30 Jan. 1766. 13 Aug. 1770.
    "In a weak and low condition.: Legatees: Mrs. Ann Turner, Lewis Ellzey
    Turner (godson), William Groves (Graves ?). Body to be buried on east side
    of Rocky Run Chapel. Mr. Wilson, now clerk, may read burial service and
    be allowed five shillings for his pains. "Desire that I may be kept four days
    before I am laid in my coffin." Exrs: Capt. William Carr Lane, Mr. Flem-
    ing Patterson. Wit: Jereimah Hutchison, Hardage Lane. (p. 252)

JOHNSON, John
    2 March 1770. 13 Aug. 1770.
    Wife: Mary Johnson. Daughter: Mary Chaney to receive 20 shillings. Exrs:
    sons Smith and Bayley Johnson. Wit: William Debell, Joseph Swain, John
    Hutchison, John Debell. (p. 253)

CHINN, Christopher
    Legatees: To brother Raleigh Dowman, five shillings. Cousin Raleigh Dow-
    man (son to William, dec'd.); nephew Christopher Chinn, son of Charles;
    John Chinn (son of brother Charles); Christopher Chinn, son of brother Eli-
    jah; brothers Charles and Elijah to receive slaves; Elizabeth Chinn (dau. of
    bro. Elijah); father Raleigh Chinn, of Lancaster Co. Exrs: brother Charles
    Chinn. Wit: Leven Powell, Thomas Chinn. (p. 254)

GOODIN, John
    14 Sept. 1769. Aug. 1770.
    "Very sick." Legatees: Samuel Goodin (son of David and Kesiah); Amos Good-
    in (brother); Martha Goodin (daughter of Amos and Sarah); Samuel and David
    Goodin (sons of Amos and Sarah); Rebecca and Sarah Goodin (daus. of Amos
    and Sarah); children of Isaac Pettet and wife Margaret, their son, John Pettet,
    to receive land in West New Jersey. Exrs: Amos Goodin and Frances Forg.
    Wit: Jonathan Reed, Elisha Mark, Peter Oliver. (p. 256)

DAVIS, Nathan
>6 April 1770. 14 Aug. 1770.
>Wife: Mary Davis. Legatees: brothers John and Enoch Davis and sisters
>Anne and Mary Evans. Will proven by oaths of John Moss and James Frier.
>(p. 260)

EVANS, John
>16 March 1770. 13 Aug. 1770
>Wife: Mary Evans. Children: Amy Anderson, Charity Perrel, Mary Evans,
>Catherine Evans, Samuel Evans, William Evans. Exrs: wife and Jacob Read.
>Wit: Jacob Bodine and Apolles Cooper. (p. 260)

BIST, John
>18 July 1769. 10 Sept. 1770.
>Wife: Martha Bist. Sons: James, Thomas and John Bist. Daughter: Rachel.
>(p. 264)

BEAVER, Thomas
>8 Aug. 1770. 8 Oct. 1770.
>Wife: Martha Beaver. Sons: Samuel, William, Thomas, Robert, Joseph,
>James and John. Exrs: William Beaver, Sr., David Carlile. Wit: Spebcer
>Clack, William Beaty, Andrew Beaty. (p. 269)

REEDER, Joseph
>17 Aug. 1770. 8 Oct. 1770
>Wife: Elizabeth Reeder. Evan Thomas (son of wife Elizabeth). Sons: Wil-
>liam (eldest), Joseph, Daniel, David. Grandsons: Elijah, Jacob, Stephen.
>Daughters: Elizabeth Lake, Mary Reeder, Elener Reeder. Exrs: sons Jo-
>seph, Daniel and David Reeder, Anthony Russell.

EVANS, Price
>5 June 1762. 9 Oct. 1770
>Of Berks Co., Pa., but now of Fairfax Co., Va. Sons: Jonathan, John and
>Oliver Evans. Daughters: Ann, wife of Sylvana Robeson: Eleanor, wife of
>John Smith, Jr.; Sarah and Mary Evans. Executrix: wife Sarah Evans. Wit:
>Lee Massey, Samuel Patterson and William Jones. (p. 272)

LAND, William Carr [Lane]
>4 Nov. 1770. 10 Dec. 1770.
>Wife: Ann Land. Sons: Pressley Carr Land and Carr Wilson Land. Daughter:
>Sally Land. Exrs: James Land and Joseph Land (brothers), William Simms
>Triplett. Wit: Thomas Cockrell, Joseph Brown and Charles Clark.

JOHN, Thomas
>13 Dec. 1770. ---
>Daughters: Rachel Reynolds, Jane Cox (of Carolina), Susannah Matthews (of
>Maryland), Mary Harris (wife of Samuel Harris). Exr: Richard Williams.
>Wit: George Gregg, Abner Howell and Owen Roberts. (p. 289)

CHINN, Elijah
>22 Feb. 1771. 11 March 1771
>Children: Rawleigh, Christopher and Elizabeth Chinn. Legatees: Rhoda Dent,
>William Dent and Mary Dent. Exrs: Thomas Chinn and Leven Powell. Wit:
>Peyton Harrison and Burr Harrison.

MEYRICK, Griffith
>24 Feb. 1771. April Court, 1771
>Wife: Susannah Meyrick. Sons: James and John Meyrick. Daughter: Susan-
>nah Meyrick. Brother James Meyrick. Wit: Jacob Wells, Caleb Greenwood
>and William Smith.

PORTER, Edward
>16 June 1770. 8 April 1771
>Wife: Mary Porter. Children: Edward, Ann Murphy, Daniel, Elias and John
>Brinkley Porter. Brother William Porter. Wit: William Porter Carrell,

Susanna Clark and Aaron Lane.

THOMAS, Humphrey
1 Feb. 1771. April 1771.
Legatees: Moses Shreve, James Shreve and Samuel Shreve (cousins). Wit:
William Russell, Samuel Clendinen. Exrs: Moses Shreve and Israel Thompson. (p. 297)

DEHAVEN, Abraham'
8 April 1771. 13 Sept. 1771.
Wife: Robetta. Sons: Jesse, Jacob, Abraham and Isaac Dehaven. Daughters:
Sarah, Hannah and Ann. Exrs: sons Jacob Dehaven and Abraham Dehaven.
Wit: George McKinney, Elias Ellis and William Dehaven. (p. 298)

EVERHARD, Jacob
28 Nov. 1770. June Court, 1771.
(Original will in Dutch) Wife: Elizabeth Everhard. Children: Jacob, Charlotta and unborn child. Exr: Nicholas Off and Adam Shoder. Wit: Nicholas Phillips, Rudolph Grecelius (?), William Wihen. (p. 300)

TODHUNTER, John
3 Nov. 1770. April Court, 1771.
Son Israel and small child, not named. Exrs: wife Margaret and son John.
Wit: Isaac Land, Josias Clapham, Henry Oxley.

MARTIAL, Joseph
12 Nov. 1770. 8 April 1771.
Wife: Rachel Martial. Sons: James, Samuel (eldest), Joseph, Robert (youngest). Daughters: Mary, Margaret, Rachel, Martha and Susannah. Exrs:
wife and John Moss. Wit: James Frier, Joseph Scott, William Fox. (p. 304)

CHILTON, George
Wife: Ann Chilton. Sons: Thomas and John Chilton. Daughters: Sarah Rozell
and Mary Chilton. Exrs: Anthony Rozell and Thomas Lewis. Wit: John Lewis, Ann Lewis, Catherine Elliott. (p. 306)

JONES, William
26 March 1771. May Court, 1771.
Wife mentioned, not named. Sons: Joshua and James Jones. Daughter: Mary
Griffith. Exr: son James Jones. Wit: J. Clapham, William Lewis, Sarah
Griffith. (p. 310)

TAYLOR, Henry, Sr.
29 March 1770. 12 Aut. 1771.
Wife: Susannah Taylor. Mention former wife's children. Sons: Walter, Joshua and Henry. Sons-in-law: William Cotton, William Williams, Thomas Harden, Notley Williams. Exrs: wife and son John (youngest). Wit: Mary Sutton
(Sulton ?), John Burk and Rhoda Burk.

FRIER, James
15 March 1771. 10 Sept. 1771.
Wife is mentioned but not named. Children: Daniel, Robert, Hannah and
Pheby Frier. Son Robert to live with uncle George Kilgore. Son Daniel to be
bound to uncle Robert Muir. Exrs: George Kilgore, John Moss. Wit: James
Marshall and John Bayles. (p. 340)

WILL BOOK "B"

MARTIN, Ralph
24 March 1772. 22 June 1772.
Wife: Mary Martin. Children: William, Joseph, John, Thomas, Ann Homan,
Sarah Castleberry, Mary Eaton. Exr: friend Irael Thompson. (p. 1)

CONN, Hugh
11 Nov. 1771. 22 June 1772.
Wife: Mary Conn. Mentions young children. Sons: Hugh Coxen Conn, eldest son, Josias (or Jonas ?). Daughter: Ruth. Children of Garrard Trammell [Conn]. Exrs: wife and Garrard Trammell, Sr.

BROWN, James
October Court, 1772. Inventory.

WYATT, Thomas
29 Oct. 1772. Nov. Court, 1772.
Wife: Margaret Wyatt. Sons: John and Edward Wyatt. Daughters: Mary Lynn, Elizabeth Hanks, Sarah Cooper. Young children: Thomas, Ruth, Abner, Margaret and Reuben. Exrs: William Williams and John Feebe. (p. 21)

WINZEL, Adam
20 Oct. 1772. Nov. 1772.
Wife: Elizabeth Winzel. Children mentioned, but only eldest son Adam named. Exrs: Frantz Richie, Henry Daub. Wit: George Shoemaker, Eva and Rudolph Bartel (?).

GORHAM, Sanford
9 Oct. 1772. 25 Jan. 1773.
Wife: Ann Gorham. Daughter: Sarah Vandever. Sons: Lamken, William, Harving. Exrs: wife and Simon Triplett. Wit: John Orr, Jane Miller, Sarah Vandiver. (p. 29)

CHILTON, Martha
20 Sept. 1772. Oct. Court, 1772.
Daughters: Sarah Chilton (eldest daughter), Nancy Chilton (youngest), Sarah. Daughter-in-law Ann Chilton, wife of son James. Grandson John Chilton, son of James. Sons: Mark and Thomas Chilton. Exr: son James Chilton. Wit: Thomas Lapon and John Chilton. (p. 31)

McILHANEY, John
27 March 1773. 10 May 1773.
Wife: Rosanna McIlhaney. Sons: Thomas, John, James. Daughters: Rachel, Hannah McIlhaney and Mary McCaney (or McIlhaney). Son-in-law James McInhaney. Exrs: wife and son James McIlhaney.

HUTTON, John
---. 9 March 1772.
Sons: John and Joseph Hutton. Granddaughter Sarah Hutton (dau. of Thomas). Executrix: wife Sarah Hutton. (p. 1)

EVANS, Elizabeth
27 Dec. 1771. 9 March 1772.
Sons: William Evans, Joshua Evans. Daughters: Anne Thomas and Mary Gardner. Daughter-in-law Mary Evans. Exrs: sons William and Joshua Evans. Wit: William Fox, James Coleman and Evan Davis.

STARK, William
1 April 1772. 13 April 1772.
Sons: William and John Stark. Daughters: Mary Miner, Susannah Cockrell, Nancy Stark, Elizabeth Stark. Exrs: wife Susan Stark and Josias Clapham.

LYLES, Eleanor
13 April 1772. Inventory.

DYAL, William
14 April 1772. Inventory.

BUCKLEY, Elizabeth [Berkley]
23 Jan. 1772. 26 May 1772.
Sons: John and Reuben. Granddaughter: Ann Linton. Daughter: Althea Han-

cock. Wit: Charles Clark and Scarlett Buckley [Berkeley]. (p. 9)

LANES, John
20 May 1772. Inventory.

JENKINS, John, Sr.
24 Dec. 1772. 18 June 1773.
Legatees: daughter Elizabeth Perry to have slaves, to be divided among her
children when they come of age. Daughter Ann Gibbs. Exrs: William Gibbs.
Wit: Daniel Jenkins and William Ballinger. (p. 46)

STEPHENS, Giles
1 July 1772. 13 Sept. 1773.
Sons: James, Thomas, Giles and Edward. Daughter Mary Cole, widow of
William. Wife: Cleo (?) Stephens. Exr: son Thomas Stephens. Wit: Joseph
Abbott, Richard Abbott, Joseph Colling (Collin). (p. 47)

POOL, Benjamin
3 July 1773. 18 Sept. 1773.
Legatees: Martha, Elizabeth, Ann, Sarah, Hannah, Benjamin and Joseph Pool
(children). Exrs: wife Rebecca Pool and son Joseph Pool. Wit: William Dillard, James Dillard and Stephen James. (p. 49)

THOMPSON, Edward
6 Feb. 1773. 12 March 1773.
"In weak state of health." Son: Israel Thompson. Son-in-law Jesse Woodward and Prudence, his wife, are to be permitted to live on plantation during
life for the care they have shown him. Daughters: Sarah, Jane and Prudence.
Exrs: son Israel Thompson and Joseph Janney. Wit: David Williams, Samuel
Chamberlain and John Chamberlain. (p. 75)

FIERST, John
16 Dec. 1773. 14 March 1774.
Wife: Sarah Fierst. Children: Elizabeth, Ann, Christian and Peter. Exrs:
wife and son Peter. Wit: Nicholas Osborne.

EVANS, Joshua
30 Sept. 1773. 9 Nov. 1773.
Wife: Martha Evans. Legatees: William Thomas (son of sister); brother Wil-
liam Evans and his son John; widow and children of brother David Evans in
Pa.; Emmett Thomas and Mary Gardner (sisters). Exrs: wife, Richard
Spurr, Robert Fryer. Wit: John Moss, Robert Scott, William Harper. (p. 77)

TOBINS, James
16th Day of 12th Month, 1774. 9 May 1774.
Wife Esther to have all estate to educate small children. Children: Sarah
Masterson, George, Thomas, Mary, Joseph, Lydia, Robert, Ruth, Naomi,
Rosannah - to have four shillings each. Exrs: wife, sons George and Thomas
Tobins. Wit: Isaac Hague, Thomas Williams and Samuel Griggs. (p. 80)

KIRK, William
23 Jan. 1774. June Court, 1774.
Legatees: Sarah Brown, wife of Mercer; Mary Brown, daughter of Mercer
Brown; Betsy Brown, wife of William Brown; daughter Mary Hughes and her
four daughters, Elizabeth, Margaret, Rachel and Mary. (p. 83)

COMBS, Andrew
25 May 1773. 14 March 1774.
Wife: Mary Combs. Children: Joseph, Andrew, John, Mailan, Israel and
Rebecca. Exr: wife and brother Samuel Combs. (p. 91)

SORRELL, Thomas
24 Sept. 1774. 8 Aug. 1774.
Wife: Elizabeth Sorrell. Sons: John Spence, Aries Sorrell, Thomas Ballard
Sorrell. Daughters: Frances Moss, husband William Moss; Hannah Stevens

11

(husband Robert Stevens); Martha Sorrell. Grandson Thomas Wilson Watson. Exrs: wife and son John. Wit: Richard Rogers and John Harris. (p. 89)

SANDS, Edmund
    27 May 1774. 13 Feb. 1775.
    Of Shellburn Parish. Wife (not named) to have one-third of all land. Daughters: Hannah Roach, Sarah Sands. Sons: Israel, Benjamin, Joseph Sands. Grandson Gideon, son of Sarah Sands. Jacob Harris (son of Ann Harris), a servant lad, to son Joseph Sands. Exrs: Isaac and Joseph Sands. Wit: James Roach and Benjamin Sands.

BAKER, Nathan
    27 Jan. 1775. ---.
    Wife: Elizabeth Baker. Children: Isaac, Joseph, Rachel, Nathan and Betty (or Billy). Exr: wife and William Baker. Wit: Thomas Mathew, Lewis Nevill, Mel Janney. Security for executors' bond: Joseph Tanny, Blackstone Janny.

FEIRST, Peter
    14 Feb. 1775. 10 April 1775.
    All estate to wife (not named) and son John (under age of fourteen years). Brother Christian Feirst. Exrs: Christian Miller, Jonathan Cunnard (friends). Wit: Robert Jamison, Valentine Mangold. Will written in German. (p. 105)

HAMILTON, James
    7 Feb. 1774. 5 May 1775.
    Wife: Elizabeth Hamilton. Sons: John, James. Daughter: Mary. Exrs: wife, William Cravens, Isaac Vandevanter [Vandevander]. Wit: Daniel Griffith and Owen Roberts. (p. 119)

HOLMES, William
    22 Nov. 1774. 12 Nov. 1775.
    "Sickly and weak in body." To son William, a plantation purchased from Samuel Mead; son Joshua to have rents and profits from mill and 50 pounds curr., when he comes of age. Daughters: Elizabeth Harris, Margaret, Mary, Rachel, Deborah and Sarah. Exrs: friends William Brown and George Tavenor. Wit: Samuel Wilks, Samuel Combs, John Updike. Samuel Wils security for executors' bond.

McCLELAN, William
    1 June 1775. 15 Aug. 1775.
    Wife Sarah to have one-third of estate. Sons: Robert and William McCleland. Daughters: Martha Murphy and Mary Beavers. Exrs: wife, William Linn, Richard Skinner and Thomas Skinner. Wit: Thomas Gorham, Nicholas Wychoff. (p. 115)

FOX, William
    12 Aug. 1771. 9 Oct. 1775.
    At decease of wife, Elizabeth Fox, estate is to be sold and divided among following children: James Fox, William Fox, Susannah Scott (wife of Samuel), Margaret Scott (wife of Robert). Exrs: Samuel Scott and James Fox. Wit: William Evans, Thomas Jackson, Evan Davis. (p. 118)

LETCH, Jesse
    25 Sept. 1775. 12 Nov. 1775.
    Legatees: Mother; sister Sarah Paxten; brother Isaac Letch. Exrs: William Beane and John Harst. Wit: Joseph Janney, Abel Janney, Jr., Jacob Janney (Quakers). (p. 119)

PALMER, John
    5 Dec. 177... 13 June 1774.
    Wife: Elizabeth Palmer. Sons: Samuel Palmer (eldest), Abel and David Palmer. Priscilla Palmer (youngest daughter). Exrs: wife and son John. Wit: John Jared, Timothy Howell, Jonathan Palmer. (p. 125)

BROOKE, Hannah
    6th Day of 1st Month, 1776. 11 March 1776.
    Legatees: sister Ruth Janney to have my silver watch, looking glass, cow and
    fifteen pounds curr.; to sister Mary Janney's children, Amos and Mocahlon,
    ten pounds curr. each; daughter Deborah, 2 featherbeds, bed spreads, suit of
    brown worsted, curtains, 2 coverlids, 2 pair of blankets, 6 pair of sheets,
    pillow cases, table cloth, towels, walnut table, blue chairs, silver spoons,
    case of drawers, 32 pounds of curr. in the hands of John Hirsh; daughter
    Elizabeth, personal estate; unto friend Ann Jones (widow) a brindled pyed cow
    and 1/3 part of my sheep; unto Fairfax Monthly Meeting, fifteen pounds of
    curr. & 20 shillings for repairing the graveyard; should daughters die without
    heirs, their part of estate to go to cousin Cornelia Janney (dau. of Abel Jan-
    ney). Exr: Mahlon Janney (brother). Wit: Joseph Janney, Ruth Janney, Mah-
    lon Janney, Ann Jones. (p. 127)

CARROLL, Demse
    No date of will. Recorded 19 May 1776.
    Wife: Rebecca Carroll. Daughters: Frances (wife of Henry ---), Rachel Car-
    roll. Mary Ann Carroll and Cynthia Carroll, Mary Owens (and her son Tho-
    mas Hogen ?), son-in-law William Smith. Exrs: wife, son-in-law Silvester
    Welch (of Fauquier Co.). Security for executors': John Orr. Wit: William
    Turner, Jr., Mary M. Porter and Henry Wiseheart. (p. 134)

BYLAND, David
    23 March 1776. 13 May 1776.
    Shelburne Parish. "Very sick and weak in Body." Daughters: Elizabeth,
    Martha, Rachel. Sons: Samuel and Jesse Byland. Son Jesse to receive his
    part of estate when twenty-one years of age, which will be May 14, 1779, and
    daughter Rachel to receive her part when twenty-one years, which will be
    May 18, 1781. Exrs: daughter Elizabeth Byland and Elias Ellis. Wit: William
    Ross, John Alexander Brown and Rebecca Dehaven. Executors' security:
    Jonathan Price. (p. 134)

WEST, Thomas
    16 Aug. 1776. 13 Jan. 1777.
    Legatees: Margaret Peyton (niece); Ann Peyton (sister); William Peyton
    (nephew), nephews Frances Peyton, Craven Peyton and Valentine Peyton;
    nieces Elizabeth and Margaret, nephew Charles West. Exrs: Craven Peyton,
    Gent. Wit: Ann Peyton, Nicholas Hychew, Jacob Hychew. (p. 142)

ELLIOTT, John
    11 Nov. 1776. Jan. 1778 (?).
    "Sick and Weak - to be buried at the Burying Ground in Leesburg near where
    Robert Ball was buried." Wife: Thomasine Elliott. Friend John Lewis.
    Exr: wife. Wit: Thomson Mason, Sarah Lewis, Levi Lewis. (p. 144)

SKILMAN, John
    28 Dec. 1776. No date of probate.
    Wife: Catherine Skilman. Children mentioned, not named. Exrs: wife and
    Gabriel Fox. Wit: Susannah Campbell, William Fox, Ann Fox.

LUTESINGER, Philip
    March, 1776. 15 April 1777.
    Wife: Sarah Lutesinger. Sons: Michael and Philip Lutesinger. Daughter:
    Rebecca. Exrs: wife and Casper Quick. John Thomas made overseer of
    will. Wit: John Thomas, Conrad Dan. (Written in German)

HOWELL, Hugh
    6 March 1777. 12 May 1777.
    Farmer. "Very sick and weak in body." Wife: Margaret Howell. Children:
    Andrew, Abner, John, Benjamin, Daniel, Reuben, Rachel and Ann Howell.
    Exrs: wife, son William, Timothy Hixen. Wit: William Hixen, Francis Hague.
    (p. 176)

HOUGH, Joseph
    26 April 1777. 12 May 1777.
    Estate to wife for maintenance and bringing up of my children. Children:
    Sarah, Brand, Coleman, Hugh and James (last three names illegible). Exec-
    utrix: wife Ann Hough. Wit: John Hough, William Hough, Jr., William Hough,
    Sr. (p. 177)

POSTON, Francis
    17 Aug. 1776. 17 May 1777.
    "Sick and in a low state of health." Wife: Sarah Poston. Sons: Francis,
    Elijah and Samuel Poston. Exrs: sons Francis and Elijah Poston. Wit:
    John Barker, James Saunders, Elijah Williams. (p. 178)

LUCAS, Alexander
    30 July 1776. 11 Aug. 1777.
    Estate to wife Cassandra (?), brother and sister. Exrs: John Littleton.
    Security: William and Charles Littleton (Illegible). (p. 179)

JOHNSTON, George
    27 Nov. 1776. 4 Aug. 1777.
    Legatees: brothers Archibald, Dennis McCarty and Wilford Johnston, sister
    Betty Johnston. Exrs: brother Archibald Johnston, Leven Powell. Francis
    Peyton security for executors. (p. 180)

HAMILTON, Robert
    14 March 1777. 11 Aug. 1777.
    Will illegible. Jane Hamilton granted administration of estate.

BRECKELL, Wright
    25 June 1777. ---.
    All estate to wife Elizabeth Breckell. (p. 185)

LANE, William
    8 Sept. 1777. Inventory.

OXLEY, Henry
    9th Day of 3rd Month, 1776. October 1777.
    Children: Henry, Henning (or Hennell) and Mary Henning. Granchildren:
    Jesse Oxley and Barthany Landin. Exrs: daughter Rachel Oxley and Joseph
    Janney. Wit: Robert Fulton, Ann Oxley, Brittain Oxley. (p. 188)

JENKIN, David
    16 Sept. 1777. 10 Nov. 1777.
    Sons: John and Isaac Jenkins. Daughters: Margaret and Mary. Exr: son
    Isaac. Wit: Icabod Lodge, William Lodge and Samuel Rich. (p. 196)

MARTIN, James
    20 Aug. 1776. 8 Dec. 1777.
    Legatees: nephew James Martin (son of William); Anthony Swick to have his
    freedom when he comes of age; Elizabeth Patten, money when she comes of
    age; nephews William and James Liken; wife Uphemia (Euphemia). Exrs:
    wife, brother William Martin, William Smith. Wit: Jacob Reed and Nicholas
    Wyckoff. (p. 201)

BUTCHER, Samuel
    12 Sept. 1769. 9 March 1778.
    Wife Susannah to have plantation, also bond of forty-two pounds, dated in
    year of 1765, from John Butcher, Sr. of Pa. Children: Samuel, John, Hannah
    Phillips, Elsie Pierce, Jane Butcher, Elizabeth. (Seven children mentioned,
    only six named.) "I give and order the bond due me from Samuel Butcher,
    Jr., in Pa., of eighty pounds, being dated 1768, to be divided among my seven
    children - Samuel and Jane youngest." Two acres of land to use of Baptist
    Meeting. Legatee: Thomas Lewelyn. Exrs: Jenkins Phillips and Benjamin
    Overfelt. Wit: James Grady, David Boulton and Peter Romine. Benjamin
    Overfelt, one of the executors refused to take oath of Allegiance and Fidelity

to the Commonwealth of Virginia, is not admitted as an executor. Jenkin Phillips, the other executor then named. Leven Powell and Stephen Rozell, security in sum of 2000 pounds curr. (p. 203)

YEATES, Samuel
4 April 1773. 18 June 1778.
Wife Johannah Yeates to have one-half of all estate and to dispose of same as she thinks best. Sons: Joshua, George and Benjamin Yeates. Daughters: Rachel Money, Mary Money and Frances Simmons. Exrs: wife and son Benjamin. Wit: Nicholas Money, John Moss, John Laid (or Said). (p. 218)

COCKERILL, Thomas
17 Jan. 1777. 8 Sept. 1778.
Cameron Parish. Daughters: Elizabeth Triplett, Anna Raney Jett (?). Sons: Jeremiah, Sanford, Thomas, Benjamin and John (Sanford, Thomas and Benjamin youngest sons). Exrs: sons Jeremiah and Sanford Cockerill). Wit: Jeremiah Hutchison, Robert Bland, John Haddocks. (p. 219)

GIST, John
7 May 1778. 5 June 1778.
Wife Mary to have all movable estate as long as she remains a widow. Sons: William, Nathaniel, Thomas, Henson Gist. Daughters: Sarah Gist, Constant Gist, Elizabeth Low, Mary Keen and Vilet Lewis. Grandson Henson Lewis Gist. Granddaughters: Elender and Elizabeth Keen. Exrs: Mary Gist, George Lewis. Wit: Joseph Lewis, James Paul, Robert Riely (Riley). Sec. for executors, William Stanhope, Joseph Lewis. Bond 3,000 pounds curr. (p. 221)

WIGGINTON, Roger, Sr.
10 March 1778. 5 June 1778.
Wife: Eleanor Wigginton. Sons: Henry, William, Benjamin, Roger Wigginton. Daughters: Mary Davis, Elizabeth and Elinor. Exrs: wife, son Henry and John Davis. Wit: John Bayles, John Jackson, Jr., S.S. Donaldson. (p. 223)

MUIR, Robert
3 Feb. 1778. 9 June 1778.
Wife, Phebe Muir, to have use of entire estate to educate and raise the children. Sons: John, George, Cato, Samuel, James and Jeremiah Muir. Exrs: trusty friend George Kilgore and John Baylis. Wit: James Marshall, James Dickey. (p. 227)

TYLER, Ann
Account of executor of Ann Tyler, dec'd. for years of 1772, 1774, 1775, 1776, and recorded. John Peake, executor.

SANDERS, James
10 April 1778. 18 Aug. 1778.
Wife Sarah to have full possession of estate during her life. Sons: Gunnell, James, John, Pressley, Henry, Moses, Aaron and Cyrus. Daughter: Barbara. Newphew Henry, if he lives to age of twenty-one years. Mentions land in North Carolina. Exrs: wife, John Sanders, Aaron Sanders. Wit: Thomas Sanders, Sarah Price and Jonathan Price. (p. 236)

LANE, William
Account of James Lane of estate of William Lane, dec'd.

BATTSON, John
22 July 1778. 14 Sept. 1778.
Wife Marhery Battson and eldest son John to have all estate with which to raise other children. Benjamin Drane to possess plantation on which he lives by paying rent for same. Wit: Richard Crupper, Thomas Gibson. (p. 238)

LEWIS, Nathan
7 March 1777. 12 Oct. 1778.
Estate to be divided among brothers and sisters. Exrs: Stephen Lewis (father)

and Israel Thompson. Wit: John Davis, Josiah White, Samuel Rich. (p. 244)

SMITH, William
4 Feb. 1778. 11 Dec. 1778.
Legatees: To son of Hannah Millan, called William Smith, sixty pounds curr.,
when he comes of age; brothers Daniel and James; sisters Mary, Alice, Jean
and Elizabeth Smith; sons and daughters of William and Jean Smith, of the
Kingdom of Ireland, in Kings County. Exrs: John Orr, Major Charles Eskridge. Wit: Ann Eskridge, Sally Lane and John Walker. "As soon as executors receive money they are requested to pay it to Col. John Fitzgerald, of
Alexandria, in Colony of Virginia, that he may send it home."

SKILMAN, John
10 Feb. 1777.
Will proved in court by oaths of Susannah Overfield and William Fox, Anna
Fox. Exrs: Catherine Skilman, Gabriel Fox. Security: William Allen, Absalom Fox.

SCOTT, Joseph
12 Nov. 1776. 10 March 1777.
"Weak and Infirm." Wife, Hannah Scott, to have personal estate and support.
Sons: Thomas, Robert and William. Daughter Martha Scott to receive fifty
pounds curr. when twenty years of age. Exrs: wife, Samuel Marshall, Oliver
Price. Wit: Samuel Scott, James Marshall, Rachel Marshall.

KEEN, John
29 June 1775. 10 March 1777.
All estate to wife Sarah, at her decease to be divided between sons Richard
and James. Daughter Mary. Grandchildren: John and Ann Keen. Ann Hopewell, daughter of wife Sarah. Exrs: wife, nephew Francis Keen, friend Anthony Russell. Wit: Andrew Smalley, Daniel Mittinger, H. J. Patten (or Potten). (p. 159)

FIELDS, Thomas
20 Aug. 1776. ---.
Of Loudoun Co., but now a soldier in Capt. Thomas Watts company. Legatees: one-half of estate to sister Eleanor Priest, but not to be under the di-
rection of her husband, William Priest; nephews Thomas and John Fields,
sons to my brothers John and William Fields. Exrs: Col. Anthony Russell
and brother William Fields. Wit: Amos Davis. (p. 162)

ROBERTS, Owen
11 Jan. 1776.
Legatees: wife Jean Roberts; son William Roberts, all land; son William to
pay daughter Catherine Pophin 40 shillings yearly, for ten years; grandson
Joseph Banon (or Burow). Exr: wife Jean Roberts.

PURSLEY, Thomas
29 March 1779. 12 April 1779.
Farmer. All land to be rented out during these troublesome times and rents
issueing from lands to be divided among my seven sons: John, Henry, Thomas, Daniel, Benjamin, Larrance, Samuel Pursley. It is my will that after
these times are over and money comes of value, that all land be sold and
money divided. Daughter Catherine - her son William to have common school
education at expense of the estate. Daughters: Mary, Christiana, Elizabeth
and Deborah Pursley. To son-in-law Richard Osburn and wife Hannah (daughter), five shillings. Exrs: Robert Jamison and James McIllhaney (friends).
Wit: Josiah White, James McIllhaney, Richard Smith. (p. 279)

MORTIMER, William
10 Jan. 1779. 12 April 1779.
Ann Geesling and Rebecca Anderson came before the Justice of Peace of Loudoun Co. and made oath that they were at the house of John Anderson the fifth
day of January and were present when William Mortimer died of small pox,
caught in the natural way, about an hour before he expired he said he wanted

his possessions to be given his mother, Sarah Mortimer, brother Infamous Mortimer and sister Bethelmere. Sarah Mortimer was granted administration on estate. (p. 281)

EVANS, Zachariah
29 Sept. 1777. 10 May 1779.
Wife: Elizabeth Evans. Son Alexander Evans (under eighteen years), daughter Jane, wife of Hezekiah Bagley, daughter Edison (?), wife of William Wigginton. Other children mentioned. Extrx: wife Elizabeth Evans. Wit: Spencer Wigginton, Lashley Wood, John Gunnell. (p. 282)

RUSSELL, Anthony
2 Jan. 1779. 8 March 1779.
Land to son Francis Russell, purchased from Thomas Elzey, also land on Broad Run. Daughter Milly Russell (eldest), land. Youngest daughter, Penelope Russell, land. To Amy Hall, daughter of Mary Hall, who is now supposed to be Mary Lake, the sum of two hundred pounds curr., when she is eighteen years of age. Exrs: Spencer Grayson and son Francis. Wit: W. Allen, Minor Smith, W.E. Urey and Daniel Mitinger. (p. 271)

SANDERS, James
Inventory. Apprs: William Douglas, William Woolard, John Todhunter.

LESE, George
24 Sept. 1778. ---.
"Sick and Weak in Body.: Wife: Dorothy Lese. Children: John, Catrean, Dorety, George, Bartholomew, Hannah, Joseph Lese. Extrx: wife Dorothy Lese.

CORNELASON, Garrett
13 Jan. 1775. 8 Feb. 1779.
Sons: John, Peter, Cornelius and Conrad Cornelason. Exrs: wife (not named), sons John and Peter Cornelason. Wit: Thomas Adams, Sarah Adams, Patrick McVey. (p. 259) (Will written in German - name spelled Cornelason and Corneluson)

WINGARDNER, Harbard
9 Sept. 1779. 11 Oct. 1779.
Son Harbard to have plantation and remainder of estate to be divided among four children: Harbard, Henry, Charity Houghman and Mary Barb. Exrs: Son Harbard Wingardner. Wit: James Jennings, Anthony Huffman. (p. 308)

OXLEY, Rachel
28 Oct. 1779. 8 Nov. 1779.
Legatees: Jesse Oxley, 1 shilling, left him by my father; son Jeremiah, two shillings; Mary Oxley (daughter of brother John), "my stricket gound"; Mary Oxley (dau. of sister Hannah), "gold ring, red pocket book"; Elizabeth Howman; sister Hannah Stevens; son Joel Oxley all estate bequeathed me by my father, Henry Oxley; "I leave Joel to James Stevens and wife Hannah." Exrs: James Stevens and John Oxley. Wit: James Stevens, Alice Stevens and Hannah Stevens. (p. 313)

RICHARDSON, James
29 June 1779. ---.
Planter. Wife and two children mentioned, but not named. Exr: William Cavin. Wit: John Richardson, James Rattekin (?). (p. 307)

HOPHPOCH, Cornelius
18 Sept. 1779. 11 Oct. 1779.
All estate to wife Alie Mary Hophpoch to dispose as she pleases. Wit: James Jennings, Michael Hiler, Thomas Moore. (p. 307)

SQUIRES, Thomas
3 Nov. 177... 14 Feb. 1780.
To wife Ann Squires, all estate during her life. Daughter Sally, 30 pounds

curr. Daughter Mary, wife to William Hancocke, five shillings. Other children mentioned but not named. Extrx: wife Ann. Wit: James Marten, Stephen Tolen, H. J. Patten. (p. 319)

NEALE, Robert
24 Nov. 1779. 14 Feb. 1780.
Legatees: Sarah and Ruth Neptune, John Neptune, Isaac Nichols, Rebecca Nichols, "to my little girl Dinah Riena," John Drane, Benjamin Hewelson. Wit: Benjamin Sands. Security for executors: Joshua Gore, Isaac Vandevinder. (p. 321)

FIELD, Thomas
13 Feb. 1778. 13 March 1780.
Wife: Jemima Field. Children: William, Thomas, John, Eleanor Priest. Exrs: sons John and William. Wit: James Hopkin, George Twiddy, Henry Patten. Security: Frances Russell and John Tyler, bond ten thousand pounds Virginia currency. (p. 323)

ALLEN, William
14 March 1776. 10 April 1780.
Soldier, "being joined in the army." Legatees: brother Joseph Allen, sisters Else, Ann and Elizabeth. Brother Joseph under eighteen years of age. Exrs: Gabriel Fox. Wit: James Frazier, William Fox. (p. 327)

COUTZMAN, Jacob
22 June 1780. 10 July 1780.
Wife: Catherine Coutsman. Children: Hannah, Louisa, Clarissa, Catherine and unborn child. Exrs: Mr. James Kirk, Samuel Murray, John Reigor, Patrick Cavans (or Cavins). Wit: William Taylor, John Harris. Executors' security: Henry McCabe, William Smith, bond 200,000 pounds curr. (Name also spelled Coutsman) (p. 328)

TALBERT, Anne
17 Nov. 1780. 11 Dec. 1780.
Children: Ann, Frances, Benjamin, John and William Talbert. Friends Benjamin and Mary Boydston to live on the plantation until son Benjamin comes to full age. Exrs: Benjamin Boydston (friend) and John Moss (brother). Wit: Cornelius Ringo, Margaret Ringo, Monica Littlejohn and Frances Minor. Security: John Minor, John Littlejohn, Benjamin Boydston, Thomas Respess, bond 200,000 pounds curr. (p. 358)

BOYD, William
21 Nov. 1780. 12 March 1781.
Wife: Jane Boyd. Children: William, Betty, Nancy, James, Thomas. Exrs: wife, John Boyd. Wit: John Minor, John Harrison, Ruth Lucas. Security for executors, John Minor. Bond 30,000 pounds curr. (p. 360)

HAGUE, Francis
24th Day of 8th Month, 1780. 13 Nov. 1780.
Legatees: To Trustees of Fairfax Meeting House, land adjoining the Meeting House; sons Isaac, Thomas and Samuel Hague. Daughters: Ann, Mary, Rebecca, Sarah and Hannah. Granddaughter: Jane Janney. Exrs: sons Thomas and Samuel Hague, Israel Thompson. Wit: Jane Roberts, Eleanor Roberts, John Hough, Andrew Brown. Security: Israel Thompson, Thomas Hague, Samuel Hague, William Douglas, Farling Ball and William Hixon. Bond, one hundred pounds Virginia curr. (p. 355)

FOUCH, Hugh
24 Sept. 1780. 14 Nov. 1780.
Wife: Mary Fouch. Sons: Zach, Jacob, Jonathan, Abraham. Granddaughter: Mary Fouch, daughter of Zach. Extrx: wife. Wit: William Brown, Joseph Morehane and Thomas Hetherby. Security: George Rine and Jacob Jacobs. Bond, eight thousand pounds curr. (p. 357)

PEYTON, Craven
    30 Oct. 1780. --- 1781.
    Wife: Ann Peyton. Sons: William, Craven, Valentine and Francis Peyton.
    Daughters: Margaret and Ann Peyton. Exrs: wife, William, (son), Francis
    Peyton (brother).

LEVERING, Septimus ,
    21 August 1781. 13 March 1782.
    Wife: Mary Levering. Children: Mary, Septimus, Griffith, Thomas and Al-
    ice. Son-in-law: James Lawrason. Exrs: James Kirk, James Lawrason.

CAMPBELL, Mathew
    23 Feb. 1782. 11 March 1782.
    Legatees: Helen Curtis (widow), Mary Curtis (daughter of Helen Curtis),
    Janney Patterson, mother Marion Campbell (widow of John Campbell). Exrs:
    James Kirk, Neilson Patrick Cavan, Robert Adams. Wit: James Wilson,
    Mary Wilson and Henry McCabe. (p. 397)

DONALDSON, Daniel
    22 Feb. 1782. 13 May 1782.
    Legatees: Jeremiah Moore (friend) and Ann Donaldson (sister). Extrx: sister
    Ann Donaldson. Wit: Stephen Donaldson, Sally Donaldson. (p. 415)

WALKER, Isaac
    10th Day of 4th Month, 1782. 10 June 1782.
    Legatees: sisters Sarah Harris, Hannah Smith, Rebecca Frahern (widow),
    cousins Sarah Frahern, James Frahern, William Frahern. Exrs: Israel
    Janney, James Frahern. Wit: Lewis Lemert, Jacob Janney, Nathan Spencer.
    (p. 416)

ROBISON, John
    19 Feb. 1782. 10 June 1782.
    Wife Sarah to have entire estate with which to bring up the children. Chil-
    dren: Elizabeth, Nancy and Sarah Robison. Exrs: Thomas Hitch, Smith King,
    Benjamin Cooper. Wit: Robert Frier, Mary Wood, Milly Wood, Lawerence
    Ward. (p. 418)

BAKER, William
    29th Day of 4th Month, 1778. 10 June 1782
    Legatees: wife and three children - Sarah, Joshua and Rachel. Exrs: wife,
    Mahlan Janney, Joseph Janney. Wit: Mahlon Janney, Samuel Janney, Abel
    Janney. (p. 419)

MOORE, Ann
    10 June 1782. Inventory.

MOORE, Ann
    16 March 1782. 8 April 1782.
    Legatees: Elizabeth Mary and Hannah Brent (daughters) and Thomas Neale
    (son). Exr: John Orr. Wit: John Orr, Charles Turley. (p. 413)

SWINK, Adam
    ---. April Court, 1782.
    Wife Rachel Swink, daughter Jane Swink and child. Mentions brothers and
    sisters, but does not name. Exrs: wife, David Potts, Sr., Jonathan Conrod.
    Wit: Ezekiel Potts, Robert Chalfant, John Thomas, James Adams. (p. 414)

MINOR, John
    14 May 1782.
    Nicholas Minor, next friend of John Minor, Gent., having been summoned to
    test the validity of a nun-cupative will of said will of said deceased, said he
    had no objections to said will, whereon William Stanhope and Thomas Minor
    being sworn, deposed that said John Minor on 4th of February last, did de-
    clare in their presence his last will as follows: that present he had made his
    children should be delivered to them. All estate to be divided equally between

wife and children. Extrx: wife Frances Minor. Security: Josias Clapham
and William Stanhope. (p. 426)

BENHAMS, John
    3 June 1781. 8 July 1782.
    Tailor, of Loudoun Co. "Son Robert should have good learning, then to learn
    my trade." Other children mentioned but not named. Exrs: Benjamin Mason.
    Wit: George Mason, Margaret Mason and Joab Rice. (p. 427)

ELGIN, Francis
    19 Dec. 1776. 10 June 1782.
    Wife: Rebecca Elgin. Sons: Gustavus, Walter, , Francis Elgin, to receive
    land. Other children: Ignatus, George, Jessy, Nancy, William, Margaret,
    Rebecca. Exrs: wife Rebecca. Wit: Benjamin Shreve, Stephen Hunt, Chris-
    topher Hunt. (p. 423)

MINOR, Nicholas
    25 April 1782. 12 Aug. 1782.
    Wife: Frances Minor. Sons: Thomas, John, Spencer, George Minor. Son
    George is beyond the seas. Daughters: Rebecca and Elizabeth Gunnell. Exrs:
    John Moss, Sr., Spencer Minor (son). Wit: John Linton, William Boyd, and
    Stewart Minor. (p. 431)

SCOTT, Samuel
    2 Oct. 1782. 11 Oct. 1782.
    Wife: Susan Scott. Sons: Robert, Samuel and James Scott. Daughters: Eliza-
    beth, Susan, Rachel, Peggy and Martha (wife of Thomas Lindsay). Wit:
    James Fox, William Moffett, and John Graham.

SWINK, John
    11 Nov. 1782. Inventory.

RUSSELL, Francis (Capt.)
    11 Nov. 1782. Inventory. (p. 444)

SCHOOLEY, Samuel
    10 May 1769. 12 Nov. 1782.
    To wife Sarah, plantation I hold by lease from William Fairfax. Children
    mentioned - John Schooley and daughter Mary Myers (there were probably
    others). Exrs: John Schooley and William Schooley (sons). Wit: William
    Brown and George Taverner. (p. 444)

SKILLMAN, John
    Executors Account, 1777. Closed and recorded 1782.

INVENTORIES BOOK "B"

EVINS, John
    1770. Inventory. Approved by court 27 July 1772.
    Admrs: Jacob Reed and Mary Evins. (p. 16)

LANCE, Peter
    18 Sept. 1772. Inventory. Appraised 28 Sept. 1772.
    Apprs: John Sigler, Philip Morgin, Peter Archer. (p. 16)

BROWN, James
    20 March 1772.
    Apprs: Richard Crupper, John Smart, James Batson.

JOHNSON, John
    29 Sept. 1772.
    Exrs: James Johnson and ... Johnson (Johnston). (p. 18)

TAYLOR, Henry
        August 1771. Inventory.
        Apprs: Thomas Shore, Nathan Smith and Jacob Reed.

MARTIN, Ralph
        24 Nov. 1772. Inventory.
        Apprs: Thomas Pursley, John Collins.   (p. 25)

SIMPKINS, John
        20 Dec. 1772. Inventory.
        Apprs: Thomas George, Richard Williams, John Steere.

CHILTON, Martha
        28 Dec. 1772. Inventory.
        Apprs: William Littleton, Henry Brewer, Thomas Self. (p. 25)

STEPHENS, Giles
        March 1774. Inventory.
        Apprs: John Lewis, William Cavins, James Sanders. (p. 72)

BURKS, Edward
        Inventory. Appraised 20 May 1774. (p. 82)

WYATT, Thomas
        December 1772. May 1773. Inventory. (p. 41)

DAYS, George
        11 Dec. 1772. May 1773. Inventory.

BROADWATER, Guy
        14 June 1773. Settlement. (p. 42)

DEHAVEN, Abraham
        Inventory. Approved by court, 15 June 1773.

CHILTON, George
        Account with Thomas Owsley, executor, approved by court, 15 June 1773.

HARRIS, William
        10 April 1773. Inventory. Joseph Combs, administrator. (p. 45)

COLEMAN, Richard
        15 Sept. 1773. Inventory. (p. 52)

STAPLETON, Thomas
        11 Nov. 1771. 11 Oct. 1773. Inventory. (p. 52)

POOLE, Benjamin
        Inventory. 11 Oct. 1773.
        Apprs: John Brown, Sol. Hoge, James Hatcher. (p. 53)

BUKLEY, Elizabeth [Berkeley]
        11 Oct. 1773. Inventory.
        Apprs: Adam Mitchell, Jacob Remey, Jr. & Sr. (p. 55)

ANTON, William
        28 April 1773.
        Apprs: William Douglas, William Taylor (p. 56)

CHINN, Christopher
        Inventory. Returned 8 Nov. 1773. Lewis Powell & Thomas Chinn. (p. 58)

TYLER, Ann
        Accounts. 1769. Approved Nov. 1773. Admr: John Peake. (p. 61)

CHINN, Elijah
        Inventory. 11 March 1771. 14 Feb. 1774. (A long account) (p. 64)

EVINS, John
        13 June 1774. Account Sale. (p. 85)

TOBINS, James
        13 June 1774. Inventory.
        Apprs: John Tribbe (or Trible), James Nixon, Samuel Gregg. (p. 86)

EVANS, Elizabeth
        13 June 1774. Inventory.

CUNARD, William
        14 June 1774. Inventory. (p. 86)

SLOAN, John
        12 Sept. 1774. Inventory. (p. 93)

STARK, William
        Inventory. Appraised by court. Sept. 1774. (p. 94)

LOWELL (or Stowell), Thomas
        10 Oct. 1774. Inventory.
        Apprs: John Heryford, Thomas Lewis and William Baker. (p. 96)

JENKINS, John
        14 Nov. 1774. Inventory. Apprs:
        Apprs: Thomas Lewis, Sr., Thomas Lewis, Jr., Nathaniel Barker. (p. 100)

JANNEY, Abel
        10 April 1775. Inventory.
        Apprs: Israel Thompson, Benjamin Purdin, Anthony Wright. (p. 108)

LAY, Sylvester
        Inventory. Appraised 8 May 1775. (p. 113)

COLEMAN, John
        12 Sept. 1774. 8 May 1775. Inventory.
        Appraisers: Stephen Rozell, Joshua Duncan, Samuel Combs. (p. 114)

KITCHENS, William
        12 April 1775. Inventory.
        Apprs: Christopher Neal, Edward Day, Nathan Barker.

SANDS, Edmund
        18 May 1775. Inventory. (p. 120)

YOUTS, John
        12 March 1776. Inventory. (p. 130)

BOYD, Williams
        April 1776. Inventory.
        Apprs: William Stanhope, William Veale, Richard Green.

McCLELAN, William
        12 May 1776. (p. 136)

BYLAND, David
        10 June 1776. Inventory.
        Apprs: Philip Noland, John Sinclair, Abra. Dehaven.

HOLMES, William
        19 Feb. 1776. 10 June 1776. Inventory. (p. 140)

WEST, Thomas
      10 March 1777. Inventory. (p. 152)

FOX, William
      10 March 1777. Inventory. (p. 155)

HAMILTON, James
      10 March 1777. Inventory. (p. 153)

BARDON, Thomas
      Nov. 1776. 10 March 1777. Inventory. (p. 166)

MORRIS, Jacob
      5 Aug. 1775. 11 March 1777. Inventory.
      Apprs: William Muirhead, Andrew Muirhead. (p. 168)

MOSS, John
      14 April 1777. Account. (p. 170)

OXLEY, Everest
      15 April 1777. Inventory. (p. 171)

FRYER, James
      15 April 1777. (p. 175)

KEEN, John
      12 May 1777. Inventory.
      Apprs: William Allen, William Musgrove, David Carlyle.

HOUGH, Joseph
      11 Aug. 1777. Inventory. (p. 184)

CORNELIUS, Garrett
      13 March 1780. Inventory. (p. 323)

CONNERS, Ann
      10 April 1780. Inventory. (p. 329)

PEW, Samuel
      10 April 1780. Inventory. (p. 330)

WILKINSON, Evan
      11 April 1780. Inventory. (p. 332)

GORDON, Robert
      11 April 1780. Inventory.
      Apprs: Benjamin Hutchison, Francis Keen, James Whaley. (p. 232)

SQUIRES, Thomas
      12 June 1780. Inventory. (p. 334)

DONALDSON, Bayley
      12 June 1780. Inventory.
      Apprs: William Muirhead, Daniel Jennings, Edward Carter. (p. 337)

FIELDS, Thomas
      12 June 1780. Inventory. (p. 338)

RICHARDSON, James
      11 Aug. 1779 - 13 June 1780. Inventory.
      Apprs: James Kirk, George Emery, Patrick Cavan (Cavin). (p. 340)

OXLEY, Rachel
      10 July 1780. Inventory.
      Apprs: William Douglas, Charles Bele, Jonathan Price.

COLOUGH, Robert
  July 1757-1761 - 10 July 1780. Inventory. (p. 346)

BATSON, James
  9 Oct. 1780. Inventory.

RAYLEY, Nathan
  11 Oct. 1779. Inventory. (p. 310)

LEWIS, Nathan
  16 Jan. 1779. 11 Oct. 1779.
  Apprs: Josiah White, John White and Samuel Rich.

GIST, John
  11 Oct. 1779. Account vs estate. Executor: George Lewis. (p. 312)

LIES (or Leis), George
  8 Nov. 1779.
  Apprs: William Stanhope, William Muirhead, Edward Carter. (p. 314)

HOPOCH, Cornelius
  8 Nov. 1779.
  Apprs: Scarlett Berkley, John Linton, William Veale. (p. 315)

GREEN, Richard
  9 Nov. 1779.
  Apprs: William Veale, John Linton, Andrew Muirhead. (p. 316)

WINGARDEN, Harbard
  10 Jan. 1780.
  Apprs: Andrew Muirhead, William Veale, Peter Brown. (p. 317)

COMBS, Elisha
  14 Feb. 1780. Inventory. (p. 321)

STONE, Henry
  14 June 1779. (p. 293)
  Apprs: John Johnson, Nicholas Faunce, Abraham Statler, Christian Crowe.

ELLIS, Robert
  14 June 1779. Elias Ellis, administrator. (p. 294)

WIGINTON, Roger
  9 Aug. 1779. Inventory. (p. 295)

RUSSELL, Thomas, Col.
  10 Aug. 1777.
  Apprs: William Allen, Joseph Lewis, Benjamin Mason. (p. 296)

WRENN, Thomas
  10 Aug. 1779.
  Apprs: Francis Elgin, Alexander McMakin, Joseph Wildmore.

WRENN, Susanah
  10 Aug. 1779. Inventory. (p. 301)

RAMEY, Benjamin
  11 Oct. 1779.
  Apprs: George Kilgore, Samuel Wood, Henry Talbert. (p. 305)

SANDERS, James
  11 Dec. 1778. Apprs: William Douglas, William Wooland, John Todhunter.

JOHNSTON, George (Col.)
  8 Feb. 1779.

Apprs: Thomas Chinn, Joseph Farrow, Richard Crupper.

MORGERTS, Philip
6 March 1779.
Apprs: George Durm (/), Robert Wright, Joseph Braden. (p. 267)

MUSGROVE, William
6 March 1779.
Apprs: Thomas Gorham, Charles Pullen, John Tyler, John Alexander, Gentleman. (p. 269)

SCOTT, Joseph
March 1779.
Apprs: James Colman, William Gunnell, Smith King. (p. 275)

LUCAS, Alexander
August 1777. 8 March 1779. (p. 276)

McCONOCHEE, James
12 April 1779. (p. 278)

EVANS, Joshua
22 Nov. 1773. Recorded 10 May 1779. (p. 284)

CAMPBELL, Robert
8 May 1779.
Apprs: Richard Spurr, James Whaley, William Sanders. (p. 286)

WIGINTON, Robert [Roger]
10 May 1779.
Apprs: James Coleman, Richard Vallandigham, Benjamin Brown.

FIERST, Peter
10 May 1779. (p. 290)

LANE, William
2 July 1777. Inventory. (p. 186)

HAMILTON, Robert
20 Aug. 1777. Inventory. (p. 189-194)

ELLIOTT, John
16 Nov. 1777. Inventory. (p. 195)

GRIFFITH, William
30 Dec. 1776. Inventory. Appraised 9 June 1777. (p. 199)
Apprs: Farling Ball, Stephen Emery, Samuel Hilt, John Cavin, John Best.

BALL, John
8 April 1768. Inventory. Recorded 9 Sept. 1777.
Apprs: John Best and John Cavins. (p. 200)

SKILLMAN, John
Inventory. Recorded 9 March 1778.
Apprs: Vincent Lewis, Benjamin Mason, William Allen. (p. 202)

MARTIN, John
9 March 1778. Inventory. (p. 208)

BRICKELL, Wright
Inventory. Apprs: William Douglas, John Lewis, Benjamin Edwards.

TYLER, Anne
8 June 1778. Account.
Accounts of John Peake, one of the executors of Ann Tyler, dec'd., for

years 1773, 1774, 1775, 1776. (p. 225)

PIERCE, John
8 June 1778. Inventory.
Apprs: Richard Thacker, John Thacker, William McKnight. (p. 228)

JENKINS, Amos
9 June 1778. Inventory. (p. 228)

WATSON, Thomas
9 June 1778. Inventory.
Apprs: William Veale, John Boyd and Samuel Smith.

RHODES, Jacob
The goods of the wife of Jacob Rhodes sold by order of the Court, 8 June 1778.
(p. 232)

JENKINS, David
17 April 1778. Inventory.
Apprs: Robert Jameson, Thomas Humphrey, Isabell Lodge. (p. 233)

BALL, John
9 Sept. 1777. Account of estate. Francis Hague, administrator. (p. 235)

LANE, James
10 Aug. 1778. Inventory. (p. 238)

LANE, James, Esq. (Major)
14 April 1778. Inventory.
Apprs: John Cockerille, William Millian, Charles Eskridge. (p. 212-214)

HARRIS, John
12 April 1776. Inventory.
Apprs: Jacob Dehaven, Abraham Dehaven, Elias Ellis. (p. 211)

SHEDD, James
15 April 1774 - 11 May 177(8). Inventory.
Apprs: Will Lane, Jere Cockerille, Amos Fox. (p. 214)

COOPER, Apollos
16 Dec. 1777.
Apprs: Thomas Shores, Richard Crupper, Richard Skinner. (p. 216)

BEYLAND, David
8 June 1778. Account.
Account presented by Rebecca Ellis, administratrix of Elias Ellis, dec'd.
who was one of the executors of David Beyland (or Bayland), to which she
made oath - which was approved by the court. (p. 223)

CONNER, Charles
10 Aug. 1778. Inventory.
Apprs: William Whitely, George Taylor and Thomas Shore. (p. 240)

BOTTS, Aaron
June Court, 1778. Inventory.
Apprs: William Ray (or Roy), James Sanders, Sr., Thomas Repess. (p. 241)

YATES, Samuel
14 Sept. 1778.
Apprs: Thomas Lewis, Mathew White, William Jenkins. (p. 242)

FRY, Henry
9 Nov. 1778. Inventory. (p. 245)

MONKHOUSE, Jonathan
    25 Sept. 1778. Inventory. (p. 249)

STREET, Martin
    14 Nov. 1778. Inventory. Apprs: Robert Wright, Joseph Braden, Jacob ---.

MOLTON, Mary
    14 Dec. 1778. Inventory. Administrator: James Sanders.

TROUT, Jeremiah
    16 Oct. 1778. Inventory. (p. 253)
    Apprs: Benjamin Mason, Vincent Lewis, Joseph Lewis, George Lewis.

MUSGROVE, William
    9 Oct. 1780. Estate Account. Administrator: Nathaniel Smith. (p. 352)

CROSS, Joseph
    Inventory. Apprs: Benjamin Mason, John Linton, Scarlett Berkley. (p. 354)

BUTCHER, Samuel
    8 Jan. 1781. Inventory. (p. 359)

O'NEALE, Ferdinand
    12 March 1781. Inventory. Apprs: John Jones, Daniel Lofton, Saml. Canby.

TALBOTT, Henry
    12 March 1781. Inventory. (p. 361-63)
    Apprs: John Jones, Daniel Loftin, Benjamin Davis, Christopher Greenup.

McCABE, Henry
    21 July 1780. 11 June 1781. Inventory.
    Apprs: Thomas Roper, Samuel Murray and John Hereford. (p. 368)

LUCAS, Samuel
    3 March 1781. Inventory. (p. 368)

WILL BOOK "C"   1783 - 1788

BODINE, Jacob
    13 Jan. 1783. Inventory.

THORNTON, John
    13 Jan. 1783. Inventory. Of Stafford County (p. 2)

MUSGROVE, William
    Estate Account. 1778-1782. 10 Feb. 1783. Admistrator: Nathaniel Smith.

PITZER, Harman
    10 Feb. 1783. Inventory. (p. 7)

BROUGHTON, William
    13 Jan. 1783. Inventory. (p. 10)

POOL, Thomas
    8 March 1782. March 1783.
    Wife: Elizabeth Pool. Children: Daniel Pool, Elizabeth Brown, Frances Pool,
    Dorothy Pool. A son-in-law is mentioned but not named. Among children
    named is Richard Hedges - a grandson or stepson. Exrs: Benjamin Mason,
    James Gibbs and Reuben Berkley. (p. 11)

TODHUNTER, John
    10 March 1783. Inventory.

DOUGLAS, William
    30 June 1780. 11 March 1783.
    Wife: Sarah Douglas. Daughters: Kitty Neale [Heale] (eldest), 300 pounds of
    curr.; Elizabeth Douglas, 300 pounds of curr.; Nancy Douglas, 400 pounds of
    curr. Sons: Hugh and Patrick Douglas. "Land to son Patrick - the same now
    going over the mountain to claim an Officer Rights which Valintine Crawford
    bought of Capt. William Christie, of Ft. Pitt." All the estate that may come
    to me from my father, Mr. Hugh Donaldson of Garralland, in the Parish of
    Cumnoug, North Britain." Other daughters: Peggy and Hannah Douglas. Or-
    dered that friend Joseph Record be cared for during life. (p. 15)

BERKELY, William
    14 April 1783. Inventory.

HARRIS, Samuel
    10 May 1782. 14 April 1783.
    Wife: Mary Harris. Sons: Thomas, Samuel and William Harris. Wit: Joshua
    Daniels, Jane Daniels. (p. 20)

FILLER (or Filles), Andrew
    Appraisal of estate. 16 Nov. 1782. (p. 21)

JONES, John
    18 April 1781. 12 May 1783.
    Wife: Martha Jones. Children: Elizabeth Fields, William, John, Joseph
    Jones. Exrs: wife and son William. Wit: John Ritchie, Isaac Hughes, Joseph
    Powers. (p. 25)

JENNINGS, Daniel
    22 April 1783. 12 May 1783.
    All estate to wife Ann, after her decease to sons Daniel and Owen Jennings.
    Exrs: Jeremiah Jennings, William Jennings, James Jennings. Wit: Spencer
    Minor, Thomas Minor, John Linton. (p. 28)

DOUGLAS, William (Capt.)
    24 March 1783. Estate. (p. 29)

SORRELL, John
    21 March 1778. 13 May 1783.
    Legatees: Thomas W. Watson, a tract of land on the Ohio; mother Elizabeth
    Sharpe; sister Patty Taylor; Spencer A. Moss. Extrx: mother. Wit: Stephen
    Emery, Thomas Roper, Joseph Monhane.

POOLE, Thomas
    12 May 1783. Inventory. (p. 34)

JONES, John
    9 June 1783. Inventory. (p. 36)

FOUCHE, H.
    9 June 1783. Inventory. (p. 38)

SCHOOLEY, Samuel
    9 June 1783. Inventory. (p. 38)

COOPER, Frederick.
    13 Dec. 1773. 8 June 1783.
    Legatees: wife Catharny, brothers and sisters. Exrs: Philip Branner, Jacob
    Shoemaker. Wit: George Shoemaker, Rudolph Cooper, Philip Branner. (p. 41)

HARTMAN, Mathias
    12 Nov. 1782. 11 Aug. 1783.
    Wife Catherine Hartman, children mentioned but not named. Wit: Jacob Stat-
    ner, Martana Eacha. (p. 45)

BALL, John
Errors in credits of John Ball estate accounts. Israel Thompson, administrator. --- 1783. (p. 45)

WALTMAN, Emmanuel
17 Sept. 1782. 8 March 1784.
Wife: Margaret Waltman. Children: Jacob, William, Michael, Samuel, George, Mary Ann Stroupe (wife of Milcher Stroupe). Wit: Adam Batterfield (Batterfelt), Mathias Smith (other names in German). (p. 70)

GARRISON, N.
9 March 1784. Estate Account. Nehemiah Garrison, administrator. (p. 71)

FOUTTS, George
30 July 1779. 10 May 1784.
Wife mentioned, not named. Children: Philip, Elizabeth, Eve, Hannah, Frederick. Grandson: George Foutt, son of Frederick. Exrs: John Connard, John Wolf, Michael Osborn, Barnard Nandeern, Jonathan Connard. (p. 80)

CLEWS, Thomas
31 July 1784. 9 Aug. 1784.
Son Joseph to have estate and pay all debts. Legatees: daughter Sarah Gose, Joshua Gose, Nathan Potts, Christiana Mead (granddaughter). Wit: Jacob Janney and Joshua Gose. Nuncupative will. (p. 84)

CLAYPOLE, Joseph
9 Aug. 1779. 13 April 1784.
Wife, not named. Children: Rebecca (wife of Jacob Reid); Mary (wife of John Bishop), James Claypole, Jacob Reid. Wit: William Brown, Richard Brown, Simeon Haines. (p. 75)

LLOYD, David
10 March 1784. 10 May 1784.
Parish of Shelbourne. Legatees: sister Joan David (hus. James), property which is in the hands of her son, Elijah David, of the State of Pennsylvania; Rebecca Griffith (hus. John), 70 pounds curr., in the hands of widow Lightfoot, she being formerly the wife of Benjamin Lightfoot, of State of Pennsylvania; John Griffith (hus. of Rebecca). Wit: John King, Joseph Cheve and Daniel Moxley. (p. 77)

CROSS, Philip
18 Feb. 1784. 21 April 1784.
Legatees: Barnett Bowers and George Boers (or Boyers). Wit: George Starkhart, Peter Peckner and William Adams. (p. 72)

FARROW, Joseph
18 May 1781. 13 April 1784.
Wife: Elizabeth Farrow. Children: Mary Ann, Sarah, William, Thornton, Joseph and Thomas Farrow, land in Prince William Co. Exrs: wife, and Richard Crupper. (p. 72)

JACK, Patrick (M. D.)
12 March 1784. 13 April 1784.
"All money arising from estate to be sent home to Ireland, to mother Nancy Jack, if not living to brother John Jack. Exrs: Samuel Hough, John Dean (or Drean). Wit: Samuel Murray, George Emery, and Joseph Gilbert. (p. 73)

MEAD, William
17 June 1780. 9 Aug. 1784.
Mentions "beloved wife." Children: Mary Brown and her sons, William, Thomas and Joseph Rhodes; Hannah Thomas; Ann; Martha Wright; Elizabeth Potts; William Mead; grandsons William Wright and Joseph Thomas. Extrx: wife. Wit: Christopher Greenup, Charles Binns, John Binns.

WHALEY, James
8 July 1784. 9 Aug. 1784. (p. 85)
Wife: Ann Whaley. Col. Henry Lee all rights to land in Prince William Co.,
Va., for which I sued John Hooe. Granddaughter Hannah Neale Talbot, daughter of Benjamin. To my children by Barbara Whaley, namely: Benjamin Talbot Remey (commonly called Ben Whaley); Jacob Remey; James Whaley; Elizabeth; Rebecca; Henry; Elijah (all named Remey, but called Whaley). To
children of William Bernard Sears, by my daughter, his wife, except Charles
Sears, the son. To children of Henry Talbot, by my daughter Barbara (his
wife). It is my will that a child's part be given the above children of Elizabeth Sears and Barbara Talbot, shall bar their respective parents from claim-
ing any part of it. Brother William Whaley. Exrs: Charles Simmons, Hardage Lane, George Summers. Wit: Benjamin Cockerill, Thomas McIntosh.

CAPPER (or Copper), Frederick
August 1784. Inventory. (p. 92)

SMITH, Henry
1st Day of 7th Month, 1782. 13 Sept. 1784.
Wife: Alice Smith. Sons: Samuel, John, Thomas, David and William. Daughters: Sarah and Ann. Exrs: wife, sons Samuel, John and Thomas. Wit:
James McIllhaney, Ezekiel Potts, Nathan Potts, William Osbourne.

SAMUELS, Shadrack
Sept. 1784. Inventory. (p. 103)

ANDERSON, John
15 Sept. 1784. Inventory. (p. 104)

PUGH, Samuel
Nov. 1784. Estate appraised. (p. 112)

HAGUE, John
13 Nov. 1784. Account. (p. 113)

WARNALL, Roby
2 Aug. 1784. 13 Jan. 1785.
Wife: Edey Warnall. Children: Ann Tucker, Drucilla Ecton, Elizabeth Sarah
Warnall, James Warnall and Thomas Warnall. Grandson: Theodore Ecton.
Exrs: William Gunnell, Francis Warnall and Edey Warnall. Wit: Gideon
Moss, Peter Foreman, William Nelson. (p. 114)

KING, John
1 April 1784. 15 March 1785.
Wife: Mary King. Legatees: heirs of daughter Ann Stephens, dec'd.; daughter Hannah Talbutt; heirs of daughter Penelope Whaley. Remainder of estate
to be divided among eight children: Eleanor Stephens, Mary Smith, Osborne
King, Smith King, Elizabeth Stephens, John King, Sarah King (now Sarah
Floyd), Winney K. Carrington, Mary Smith (hus. John), Joseph Stephens
(hus. of dau. Elizabeth). Exrs: sons John and Osborne. Wit: Edward and
Sarah Rinker. (p. 119)

LAY, Abraham
28 Oct. 1784. 12 April 1785.
Sons: Abraham, Emmanuel, Joseph, Stephen Lay. Daughters: Prudence Elzey (hus. John), her children Lewis & Lydia; Lydia Richards (hus. William);
Helen Hereman (hus. William); Abigail Payne (hus. Sanford); Lena Jenkins
(hus. John); Athesia Self (hus. Presley); Sylvanus Jenkins, to inherit negro
should Athesia Self die, Sylvanus is son of Athesia Self by ... Grandson Marmaduke Lay, son of Sylvania Lay, dec'd., to receive a slave, should he die
the slave is to go to his sister (dau. of Sylvania). Wife: Sarah Lay. Exrs:
sons Abraham, Emmanuel and Stephen Lay. Wit: William Powell, Mary
Evans and Nicholas Money. (p. 121)

NOLAND, Philip
26 Oct. 1783. 15 March 1785.
Son Philip Nelson Noland, 100 pounds of curr. Children are to be liberally educated. Daughter Sall to have slave when eighteen years of age. Children: Thomas, Eneas, Sarah and Nancy. Exrs: wife and brother Thomas. Wit: Molly Ann Luckett, Patrick Jack, Josias Clapham, Willie Awbrey, Saml. Awbrey.

LOVATT, Daniel
29 March 1785. 9 May 1785.
Wife: Sarah Lovatt. Sons: David, 150 acres of land; Joseph, Jonathan, Daniel. Daughters under age of eighteen: Martha Grigg, Elizabeth, Letisha, Sarah, Likia. Sons: Elias and Edmund under twenty-one years of age. Wife to receive back rent from estate of John Dillion and Solomon Hogue, Jr. Exrs: wife and sons Joseph and Jonathan Lovatt. Wit: Joel Lewis, Amos Edwards, George Lewis, David Goodin, Samuel Goodin. (p. 136)

SCOTT, Sam
19 April 1783. 13 June 1785. Inventory.
Apprs: Jonas Colman, Joseph Gardner, Smith King. (p. 139)

BOGGES, Henry
21 May 1785. Inventory.
Apprs: Richard Vallandingham, Benjamin Brown, Ignatus Wheeler. (p. 142)

WHITACRE, George
19th Day of 5th Month, 1785. 12 Sept. 1785.
Wife: Ruth Whitacre. Sons: Joshua (to have tract of land when twenty-one years of age), Robert, Enuck, Caleb, George, Benjamin, Joseph Whitacre. Daughters: Martha, Elizabeth, Neomy, Ruth. Exrs: wife, brother Caleb, son Joshua. Wit: William Smith, Caleb Whitacre, James Dillon. (p. 147)

GORE, Joshua
6 March 1785. 12 Sept. 1785.
Sons: Thomas, Joshua and Jonathan. Legatees: William Osborne and heirs. Daughter Betsy. Wife mentioned, not named, former husband was Harry Rector. Should differences arise between Joshua and Jonathan (sons) the same to be decided by Thomas Gore and William Osborne. Exrs: sons Joshua and Jonathan. Wit: Abner Osborne, James Kitchen, Isaac Brown, William Neilson. (Name is spelled Gore and Gorr)

WHALEY, James
Account with William Lane, executors 1784.

JANNEY, Samuel
10th Day of 5th Month, 1778. 12 Sept. 1785.
Legatees: brothers Abel and John Janney, sisters Mary Baker, Sarah Hooten, Rebecca Janney, mother Sarah Janney, to receive fifty pounds of currency. Exrs: brothers Joseph and Abel Janney. Wit: Joseph Moffett, Amos (or Amon) McLaughlin. (p. 156)

THORNTON, John
Feb. 1780. Recorded 10 April 1780.
To wife Catherine, land, chariot, 4 chariot horses. Sons: Anthony, Benjamin, Berryman, Thomas and unborn child. Mentions land in Gloster Co., Va. Daniel Miller to continue as overseer of plantation. Exrs: Seth Thornton (of Carolina Co.), John Telliafero (King George Co.), Samuel Triplett, Samuel Love (Loudoun Co.). After writing will a son was born to John Thornton and wife Catherine, named William Thornton. (p. 158) Of Stafford Co.

CANTON, Mark
27 July 1785. 10 Oct. 1785.
To wife Elizabeth Canton, two-thirds of the estate on the western waters. Infant daughter Sarah. Exrs: wife, Daniel Feagan. Wit: William Cocke, Daniel Jackson, Stephens Combs. (p. 168)

SORRELL, Reuben
    29 May 1785. 14 Nov. 1785.
    (Name spelled Sorrell and Sorrill) Mentions land received from the estate of
    the late Mr. Thomas Newman which I have at reversion at the death of Mrs.
    Elizabeth Newman relict of said Thomas. Children mentioned but not named.
    Exr: Mr. Thomas Newman. Wit: Jacob Brasfield, John Chapman, William
    Collinger. (p. 173)

BRENT, George
    15 Sept. 1785. 14 Nov. 1785.
    Sons: Thomas, Willis, Martin, Hugh. Daughters: Sarah and Caty Brent.
    Exrs: wife and James Lewis. Wit: James Bartlett. (p. 175)

CURRAN, John
    15 Nov. 1785. Inventory.
    Apprs: Jesse Taylor, Joseph Burgoyne, Samuel Irvin. (p. 177)

BROWN, William
    13 Sept. 1773. 12 Dec. 1785.
    Legatees: nephew George Brown (son of John); George Brown (son of Thomas),
    nephew John Brown, great coat, velvet breeches, silver knee buckles; nephew
    Isaac Brown, white coat, velvet jacket, belt, buckskin breeches; bro. John
    and bro. Thomas Brown, millright & tools; niece Catherine; sister Hannah.
    Exrs: brothers John and Thomas. Wit: James Nickolls, John Gregg, James
    Craige. (p. 182)

BARKLEY, Barbara
    28 Jan. 1785. 12 Dec. 1785.
    Sons: John Reade, William Reade, Reuben Reade, Benjamin Barkley. Daugh-
    ter: Ann Ward. Exrs: son Benjamin and daughter Ann. Wit: William Dunbar,
    Jr., Barbesheba Haden, John Haden, Thomas Millane (Millan). (p. 184)

STEPHENS, Richard
    31 Jan. 1785. 12 Dec. 1785.
    Wife: Eleanor Stephens. Sons: Robert and Richard Stephens. Granddaughter:
    Eleanor Stephens (dau. of son Richard). Extrx: wife. Wit: John King, Jr.,
    Welden Watson, Susan Watson. (p. 187)

PHILLIPS, Jenkins
    14 Oct. 1785. 9 Jan. 1785 (?)
    Wife: Hester Phillips. Five shillings to each of following named children:
    Thomas, Samuel, Benjamin, Sarah. Grandchildren: Israel Phillips, Benja-
    min Phillips, Nancy Phillips, Sarah Phillips and Hester Phillips. Exrs: wife
    and Abner Osborne. Wit: Stephen Gregg, Isaac Jenkins, Jacob Shavor, Mary
    Hough. (p. 189)

OULDAKER, Henry
    31 Aug. 1773. 8 Aug. 1785.
    Wife: Enor Ouldaker. Sons: Abner, Henry, Isaac, William and John. Son-
    in-law John Dyer, who married daughter Hannah, dec'd. Daughters: Mary
    Lewellin, Rebekka Burson, Eleanor Ouldaker. Exrs: sons William and John
    Ouldaker. Wit: Daniel Hough, William Smith, James Lybold. (p. 192)

BAKER, Philip
    3 Jan. 1786. 16 April 1786.
    Wife mentioned. Children: Samuel, Mary Ann, Catherine, William, Hannah,
    Barbaray, Jacob, Christian, David (10 children). Wit: Adam Householder,
    Benjamin Purdon, Adam Axline. (Written in German)

HEWSTON, Benjamin
    11 April 1786.
    Nuncupative will. Proved by the oaths of Andrew Myers and John Henry.
    Legatees: Robert Short, Alice Short (wife of Robert) and her daughter Ander-
    son; Susannah Short; Sarah Short; Rebecca Short; John Threlkill.

MARKS, Isaiah
    21 Jan. 1785. 8 Aug. 1785.
    Legatees: brother and sister. Brothers: Elisha, John, Thomas, Abel. Sister Uncie Williams and her two oldest sons. Cousin John Humphrey and his brother Thomas Humphrey. Brother-in-law Thomas Humphrey. Exrs: Thomas Humphrey, Elisha Mark. (p. 194)

WILLIAMS, William
    18th Day of 3rd Month, 1780. 13 April 1786.
    Wife: Elizabeth Williams. Sons: John Williams (eldest), Abner Williams. Daughters: Hannah Williams, Elizabeth Williams. Mother, sister Rehoboth Williams. Children to receive inheritance when twenty-one years of age. Wit: Benjamin Steer, Abraham Smith, Joel Lewis, Henry Williams. (p. 197)

SMITH, Samuel
    25 Oct. 1785. Inventory.

NEWELL, Sarah
    17 Aug. 1784. 11 Sept. 1786.
    Son: John Newell. Daughters: Rachel, Seble Newell. Susan, daughter of William and Margaret ---. Sarah Newell Fletcher (gr. dau.) daughter of William and Nancy Fletcher (dau.). Wit: Stephen Jenkins, Priscilla Jenkins, James Watkins. (p. 218)

LAWERENCE, Moses
    1 Oct. 1786. Inventory.

JANNEY, Jacob
    7th Day of 3rd Month, 1786. 9 Oct. 1786.
    Daughters: Rebecca Gregg, Phebe Bennett, Hannah. Sons: Blackstone, Jonas, Joseph, Israel, Aquilla, Elisha and Thomas. Sister-in-law Margaret Pryledieu. Grandsons: Moses, Jacob Janney (sons of Jacob). Wife, not named. Exrs: sons Blackstone and Israel Janney. Wit: Mahlon Janney, Jonathan Lovett, William Kenworthy. (p. 227)

WALKMAN, Emmanuel
    9 Oct. 1786. Inventory.

BURSON, George
    3rd Day of 8th Month, 1786. 9 Oct. 1786.
    Wife: Sarah Burson. Sons: James, Joseph, Benjamin, Jonathan. Daughter: Ruth Romine, Hannah Bradfield, Esther Cunnard. Exrs: sons James and Jonathan. Wit: Joseph Gregg, Thomas Brom, William Dillon. (p. 238)

WEST, Charles
    29 Jan. 1777. 8 Jan. 1787.
    Daughters: Elizabeth and Anna Brown West. Nephew: Charles West. Legatee: Mr. John Tyloe. Exrs: Craven Peyton, John Tyler. Wit: John Tyler, Thomas Holton (or Hatton), Patrick Fenly. (p. 242)

OSBOURNE, John
    30 Sept. 1786. Jan. 1787.
    Wife: Sarah Osbourne. Sons: Richard, Samuel and William Osbourne. Daughters: Ann Gore, Sarah Pursel. Exrs: sons Richard, William, and Thomas Gore. Wit: John Thomas, Nathan Potts, Barnard Vanderen. (p. 244)

OLDACRE, Henry
    8 Jan. 1787. Inventory.

HALLING, John Wilcoxen
    20 Oct. 1786. 8 Jan. 1787.
    Estate to be kept together until 1793. Sons: William and John. Mentions son by present wife. Extrx: wife Jemima. Wit: P. Clapham, Samuel Sinclair, John Sinclair, Jr. (p. 250)

LUCKETT, Thomas
27 Dec. 1786. 12 Feb. 1787.
Wife: Elizabeth Luckett. Sons: Otho (eldest), Val, land bought of brother
John Luckett in Montgomery Co., Md., Lawson and a young son not baptised.
Exrs: wife and Reason Davis (Washington Co., Md.) (p. 253)

AWBREY, Thomas
30 Aug. 1784. 8 Jan. 1787.
Wife: Jemima Awbrey. Sons: William, Thomas, Richard, Philip, Samuel,
Henry. Mentions Rhoda and brother John. Daughter Jemima. Brother Samuel. Exrs: sons Francis and Henry. Wit: William Smith, John Davis, Susannah English.

SCHOOLEY, Samuel
23 Sept. 1786. 9 April 1787.
Children: Ann, Jesse Schooley. Exrs: wife Dorothy and brother John Schooley. Wit: Josias Clapham, John Bagley. (p. 264)

SONGSTER, John Dr.
14 Aug. 1787. Inventory. (p. 278)

LANE, James Hardage
25 May 1787. 10 Sept. 1787.
Wife: Mary Lane. Children: John, William, George, James H., Daniel C.,
Enoch Smith Lane, Mary, Rebecca, Delilah Lane. Daughters: Elizabeth
Beach (hus. Joel Beach), Sarah Darrell. Exrs: wife, son James. Wit: Isaac
Hutchinson, Coleman Brown and Charles Eskridge. (p. 280)

MONIES, John
25 Feb. 1786. 10 April 1787.
"I cut off my daughter Jennie Headon, by my first marriage, leaving her one
shilling - she has received her share." Wife Nancy and her children. Exrs:
Col. Charles Eskridge, James Hardage Lane. Wit: John Orr, Anna Gooding,
Samuel Headen, Isaac Hutchinson. (p. 284)

JENKINS, Philip
10 Sept. 1787. Inventory. (p. 287)

RAMEY (Remey), John, Sr.
4 Dec. 1784. 10 Sept. 1787.
To son Jacob, who married Elizabeth Lane about 1776-1777, to receive a tract
of land. Grand son Jacob Ramey (called Gilson Whaley), son of daughter Barbara, the present wife of William Whaley. Exrs: friend Samuel Love, Jr.
and Jeremiah Cockerille. Wit: George Summers, Charles Turley, John Whaley. (p. 288)

REAMY (Remey), Sanford
9 Dec. 1787. 4 Feb. 1788.
Legatees: Sanford Reamy Connally, John Donaldson Connally, Ann Sanford
Conally (dau. of Sanford M. Conally and wife Mary), John Conally (son of S.
R. Conally), sister Mary Corder, William Conally (son of Sanford R. Conal-
ly), Judith Corder. Heirs of brother John Remey, dec'd. Exrs: Sanford R.
Conally, John Donaldson Conally. Wit: Richard Spurr, William Whaley, Bry-
an Allison, Jonathan Pike.

LUCKETT, Thomas Huzza
17 Feb. 1787. Inventory. (p. 317)

WILLSON, John
10 July 1787. 14 April 1788.
Formerly of City of London in old England." Wife: Mary Willson. Children:
John Jeff, Henry Lawerence, Maria and Kezia. Extrx: wife. Wit: James
Dillon, Isaac Hook, Mary Hook. (p. 321)

MARKS, John, Sr.
    31 Jan. 1787. 4 April 1788.
    Wife: Ureah (or Miriah). Sons: Elisha, John Thomas and Abel. Daughters:
    Mary Humphreys (hus. Thomas), Martha Howell (hus. William), Ureah Williams
    (hus. Jenkins). Wit: John Hatcher, Philip Thomas, David Thomas. (p. 324)

HAGUE, Francis.
    10 Sept. 1787. Account. Israel Thompson, executor. (p. 296)

BERKELEY, Reuben
    29 June 1787. 8 Oct. 1787.
    Wife: Catherine. Children: George, Susannah, Fanna Rogers Berkley, Cath-
    erine Berkley, William and Ann Berkley. Children: Burgess Berkley, Eliza-
    beth Hutchison (wife of George Hutchison), Nancy Berkley, Benjamin Berkley,
    Moses Berley. (The name spelled Berkley, Berkeley) (p. 301)

PYOTT, John
    25 May 1787. 10 Sept. 1787.
    Sons: John and Amos. Daughters: Susannah Taverner and Rebekka McElroy
    (hus. Daniel). Exrs: Jonathan Myers. (p. 304)

MEAD, Ellen
    3 Dec. 1785. 10 April 1787.
    Daughters: Hannah Thomas, Mary Brown, Ann Mead, Martha Wright, Eliza-
    beth Potts, to have all land in Pa. "which fell to me by decease of sister Mar-
    tha Brown." Exrs: Anne Mead (daughter) and Ezekiel Potts (son-in-law). Wit:
    Charles Binns, Jr., George Hammat, Ralph Homasn. (p. 268)

OSBORNE, Nicholas
    17 Aug. 1785. 12 June 1787.
    Wife: Mary Osborne. Daughters: Massey Castleman, Lydia Osborne. Son:
    Abner. Grandson: Nicholas Osborne. Exrs: Abner Osborne, Duncan McClain
    (friend). Wit: Jeremiah Moore, Valentine Peyton, Isaac Brown, Mary Os-
    borne. (p. 275)

ROMINE, Peter
    20 Feb. 1787. 14 April 1788.
    Wife: Abigail Romine. Sons: John and Peter Romine. Daughter: Sarah.
    Exrs: sons John and Peter Romine. Wit: Joseph Hutchison, Stephen Shipman,
    John Popkins. (p. 335)

GREGG, John
    2 Dec. 1778.
    Children: Amos (eldest), Mary Gregg, Hannah Dixon, Amy Gregg, Lydia
    Howell, Rebecca Gregg, George Gregg, John Gregg, Richard Gregg, Levy
    Gregg (grandson). Exrs: sons George, John and Richard Gregg. Wit: James
    Adams, Isaac Hague, George Gregg, Samuel Gregg. (p. 338)

CLEVLAND (Cleavland), William
    7 Oct. 1787. June 1788.
    All estate to wife Mary, also named as executrix. Daughter: Darkes. Wit:
    Amos Fox, George Fox, Benjamin Cockerille, E. Gardner. (p. 342)

COTTON, William, Sr.
    30 June 1787. 1788.
    Wife: Mary Cotton. Sons: William and John Cotton. Daughters: Margaret
    Ghorman, Frances Spurr. Exr: son John Cotton. Wit: John Alexander, Rich-
    ard B. Alexander and John Brown. (p. 355)

CHILTON, Steerman
    14 Nov. 1784. 12 April 1785.
    Wife: Mary Chilton. Sons: John, William and Thomas Chilton. Daughters:
    Ann Cockerille, wife of John Cockerille; Agatha Williams, wife of Joshua
    Williams; Jemima Smith, wife of Gideon Smith; Sarah Chilton. Brother John
    Chilton may have sons William and Thomas, if he will take them. Exrs: wife,

son John Chilton. Wit: Christopher Cockerille, Jonathan Jewell, John Graham. (p. 126)

MURPHY, Michael
17 Oct. 1777. 12 April 1785.
"To whom it may concern - a foot soldier, being enlisted under Lieutenant Abraham Warford in the Continental Establishment on the 1st day of September, 1777 - being entitled to one hundred acres of land, I appoint Job Warford sole and lawful heir." Test: David Carlile. (p. 128)

LANE, William Carr
12 April 1785. Estate in account with Simon Triplett.

WHALEY, James
1784. Account with William Lane, Executor.

BOOK "D"

HOGUE, John
Oct. 1788. Estate in account with William Mead, executor.

SEYBOLD, Jesper
17th Day of 5th Month, 1788. 13 Oct. 1788.
Wife Rebakah Seybold. Sons: James, Isaac, John, Robert, Jesse, Silas and Jesper Seybold. Daughter Hannah and her daughter Hester. Exrs: sons John and Jesper Seybold. Wit: John Hirst, Mary Hirst, John Preston. (p. 2) Signed in German.

WILSON, John
3 May 1788. Inventory.

KITCHEN, William
3 Dec. 1780. 13 Oct. 1788.
Sons: Daniel and Thompson Kitchen. Wife: Margaret Kitchen. Mentions daughter and her husband, but does not name. Exrs: wife and son Daniel Kitchen. Wit: William D. Bell, Mary Bell. (p. 5)

HUTCHESON, William
13 Oct. 1788. (p. 7)

EVANS, Mary
20 Dec. 1787. 10 Sept. 1789.
Sons: William and Samuel Evans. Daughters: Sarah Smith, Anney and Charity. Gr. daughter: Osse Reed. Son-in-law Samuel Henderson to receive 400 acres of land in Hampshire Co. Grandson: Samuel Henderson. Legatee: John Bodine, son of Benjamin Rightmire's wife (relation not stated). Exrs: John Tyler, Francis Peyton. Wit: Benjamin Moore, John Moore, Adrian Swart. (Will signed in German) (p. 10)

BUCKLEY, William
12 July 1786. 8 June 1789.
Legatees: sons John, Samuel, Joshua, Elizabeth Harris, Sarah Harris, Catherine Harris, Rosannah Halbert, Elijah Buckley (son of William Buckley). Exrs: sons John and Joshua. Wit: Richard Neale, Richard Blackburne, John Dudley. (p. 36)

HELM, Meredith
8 June 1789. Inventory. (p. 37)

EVANS, Mary
8 June 1789. Inventory. (p. 40)

WEST, C.
8 June 1789. Inventory. (p. 44)

STEPHEN, Martin
    6 June 1789. Inventory. (p. 53)

HUMPHREY, William
    9 June 1789. Inventory. (p. 53)

CARTER, John
    9 June 1789. Inventory. (p. 76)

KITCHEN, William
    13 July 1789. Inventory.

TAYLOR, William
    27 March 1782. 9 Feb. 1790.
    After decease of wife estate to be divided into three parts - Jemimy Bogess,
    Richard Davis and Mary Whealer's three children. Wife not named. Exrs:
    son William Taylor. Wit: Handley Taylor, Demse Carroll, Jesper Seybold.

TAYLOR, George
    23 Feb. 1788. 14 Sept. 1789.
    Children: George Taylor, Hizziah Fielder, Elizabeth Squires, Frances Cot-
    ton, Stephen Taylor. Grandson: William Cotton (son of Frances Cotton).
    Mildred Compton (housekeeper) to have support for herself and three children,
    Cybitha Taylor (alias Compton), Jack T. Taylor (alias Compton), Craven
    Taylor (alias Compton). Exrs: sons George and Stephen Taylor. Wit: Tho-
    mas Fouch and Isaac Fouch, Jr. (p. 91)

HOGES, William
    13th Day of 4th Month, 1789. 13 July 1789.
    Sons: George, Zebulon, James, William, Solomon (son-in-law of Isaac Nick-
    olls). Step-daughter-in-law, Sarah Pancoast. Daughter-in-law Hannah
    Boone. Brother James Hoge. Grandson Morgan Hoge. Granddaughter Sarah
    Gore, grandson Solomon Hoge (weaver), who is my son James Hoge's own son,
    and granddaughter Nancy Jenkins (widow). Daughter Nancy Hays (hus. Wil-
    liam). Exrs: son Solomon and his son-in-law Joshua Gore. Wit: William
    Kenworthy, Joseph Shields and Rebekah Hoge. (p. 98)

RATCLIFF (Radcliff), Edward.
    4 Dec. 1789. Inventory. (p. 105)

JAMES, Elias
    20 May 1789. --- 1789. (p. 102)
    Wife: Anne James. Sons: Thomas, Isaac, James, Elias James (last two men-
    tioned as younger sons). James Nickols, who married dau. Anne, now dec'd.
    Daughter Hannah James. Exrs: son Thomas, Abner Osborne (friend), Owen
    Thomas. Wit: James Carrell, Thomas Humphrey, Jr. Thomas Humphrey.

BAYLEY, Joseph
    15 May 1789. 13 July 1789.
    Wife: Elizabeth Bayley. William and Robert Bayley (sons of brother William),
    land in Md. Children of brother Pierce Bayley, Mountjoy and Samuel Bayley.
    Brothers William and Pierce Bayley. Wit: Thomas Lewis, William Rust,
    John Triplett, Elizabeth Taylor and Eliner Holland. (p. 107)

HOLMES, William
    9 Feb. 1790 (?). Inventory. (p. 117)

MYERS, Jonathan
    25th of 3rd Month, 1780. 11 Feb. 1790.
    Wife: Mary Myers. Daughter: Esther Pierpoint. Sons: Isaiah, Elijah, Jo-
    siah. Exrs: wife, sons Isaiah and Elijah. Wit: James Moore, Thomas Moore,
    Jr. and Ann Moore. (p. 117)

PAYNE, Benjamin
    10 Feb. 1790. Inventory. (p. 118)

BROOKS, Hannah
    1790. Account with Mahlon Janney, executor. (p. 126)

GORE, Thomas
    25 Dec. 1789. 10 May 1790.
    Wife: Anne Gore. Sons: Joshua and Mark Gore. Daughters: Elizabeth and
    Hannah. Exrs: Joshua Gore (friend) and Abner Osborne (friend). Wit: Wil-
    liam Osborne, Duncan McLean and Mary McLean. (p. 132)

MOORE, William
    10 May 1790. Inventory.

WALLENTINE, George
    30 June 1790. 12 July 1790.
    Legatees: Elizabeth and Catherine Wallentine. Exrs: wife Mary, John Tylor,
    John Moore. Wit: Price Bayley, Jacob Moore, Benjamin Moore. (p. 137)

PIKE, Jonathan
    28 Dec. 1790. Inventory. (p. 143)

GIBSON, Ealse
    13th Day of 6th Month, 1787. 13 Dec. 1790.
    Sons: Isaac, Joseph, Thomas, John, James and Moses. Daughters: Ann
    Clerk (Clark ?), Rebekka Nichols. Granddaughters: Ruth (dau. of son Mo-
    ses), Miriam Gibson (dau. of William), Ealse Gibson (dau. of Isaac), Jona-
    than, Aaron, Dinah, Rachel, Susan and Jesse Gibson - children of son Moses,
    Exrs: sons Moses and John Gibson. Wit: Abel Janney, Edward Rees and Sam-
    uel Wilks. (p. 145)

KING, Mary
    14 Oct. 1790. 13 Dec. 1790
    One shilling each to sons Osborn, Smith and John King. Legatees: Sarah
    King, wife of William Floyd; Winny King, wife of Timothy Carrington; Eliza-
    beth King, wife of Joseph Stephens - daughters. Heirs of daughter Eleanor
    Stephens, Hannah Talbott, Penelope Whaley. Daughter Mary Smith. Unto
    children of daughter Elizabeth Stephens, one-half of the property. Husband
    of Mary King, John King, deceased. Exrs: grandson Joseph Stephens and
    William Whaley. Wit: William Powell, Mary Gordon, Ann Powell. (p. 148)

STEPHENS, Eleanor
    13 Dec. 1790. Date of will 2 Dec. 1790.
    Nuncupative will, proved by oaths of Mary Gordon and Robert Perfect. Leg-
    atees: sons Richard and Robert Stephens and two daughters, not named.

REED, Jonathan
    16 Feb. 1788. Jan. Court, 1791.
    Wife: Susannah Reed. Legatees: grandson Johathan Reed (son of Stephen),
    Jobe (or John) Abit (son of wife), sons Andrew, Cornelius and Stephen Reed.
    Daughters: Martha Poulton, Eunus (Eunice), Naomi and Elizabeth Reed,
    Charity Philips and her children - Sarah, Benjamin, and Nancy Philips.
    Exrs: sons Cornelius and Stephen Reed. Wit: Thomas Marks, Richard Roach,
    John Poulton. (p. 150)

NICKOLS, James
    27th Day of 12th Month, 1785. 14 Feb. 1791.
    Sons: James, Nathan, George and Isiah Nickols. Legatees: daughter Hogue
    (wife of Isaac), dau. Charity Nickols, grandson Nathan Nickols, granddaugh-
    ters, Mary Nickols, Ann Nickolls, Solomon Nickols. Exrs: son George and
    son-in-law Isaac Hogue. Wit: John Thatcher, Richard Thatcher and Daniel
    Bartlett. (p. 153)

BAYLEY, Elizabeth
    Dower. March Court, 1791. (p. 174)

ROBERTSON, William
9 Oct. 1790. 14 Feb. 1791.
Daughters: Susannah Robertson, Elizabeth Naomi, Mary Freeman, Ann Dillard, Elizabeth Newman. Sons-in-law: George Newman, John Dillard, Hezekiah Freeman. Exrs: Susannah Robertson and George Newman. Wit: Richard Newman, Joseph Newman, James Wigginton. (p. 155)

SHORT, John
9 Jan. 1787. 14 Feb. 1791.
Wife: Catherine Short. Eldest daughter Eve Clarke (?) and her son John; daughter Elizabeth Spoon. Exr: son Jacob Short. (p. 159)

EBLIN, Peter
nuncupative. 18 Dec. 1790. 10 Jan. 1791.
Legatees: children of brother John, to-wit: Samuel, John, Isaac, Hannah, Elisha, Mary and Sarah. Exrs: wife Janet, Joseph Braden. Wit: John Dodd, Joseph Gore, Philip Hide made oath that this was the Will and Testament of Peter Eblin. (p. 159)

CHAMBLIN, William
4 Feb. 1791. 11 April 1791.
Wife: Sarah Chamblin. Sons: John, Charles, William Chamblin. Daughters: Margaret Botts (hus. Archibald), Sarah Botts (hus. Moses), Elizabeth Palmer (hus. Abel), Jane Eleanor and Ann. Exrs: son John and Charles. Wit: James Rose, Peter Matthews, Dorothy Thomas. (p. 170)

CLAGETT, Charles
21 Feb. 1791. April Court, 1791.
Children named - Thomas, Monica and Mary Ann. "Estate to be divided among all my children." Exr: son Thomas Claggett. Wit: Josias Clapham, Benjamin Mackall, John Kelly. (p. 173)

NIXON, Jonathan
May 1791. Inventory.
Apprs: George Nixon, Samuel Combs, Abel Janney. (p. 180)

BURSON, Benjamin
15th Day of 12th Month, 1790. 11 July 1791.
Wife: Hannah. Sons: George and Silas, to receive tract of land. Daughters: Sarah and Catherine Burson. Exrs: wife and friend James Trahern. Wit: Jonathan Burson, Thomas Brown. (p. 188)

WHITE, Richard
20 April 1791. 11 July 1791.
Wife: Rebekah White. Sons: Benjamin, William, Daniel, Joseph, Samuel White. Exrs: wife, sons Benjamin and Daniel. Wit: Samuel Combs, George Nixon, Abel Janney. (p. 190-192)

POOL, Rebekah
4th Day of 11th Month, 1784. 12 Sept. 1791. (p. 193)
Children: Joseph, Martha, Elizabeth, Ann, Hannah, Sarah, Mary, Benjamin and Israel Pool. Wit: Benjamin Head, Caleb Whitacre, George Fanihevist.

JANNEY, William
12th Day of 6th Month, 1787. 12 Sept. 1791.
Wife: Elizabeth Janney. Sons: Jesse, Stacey, William and Isaac Janney. Daughters: Ann White, Elizabeth Hughes, Letitia Wildman. Wearing apparel to be divided between son Isaac and son-in-law Abraham Wildman. Exrs: Macey (or Stacey) and Jesse. Wit: Blackstone Janney, Elisha Janney. (p. 195)

PRICE, Thomas
Sept. 1790. 12 Sept. 1791.
All estate to wife Susannah Price. Wit: John Luckett, Samuel Clapham and Josias Clapham. (p. 200)

BROUGHTON, William
　　25 Oct. 1790.
　　Elizabeth Bayley, late Elizabeth Broughton, account of sale of estate of her
　　husband, William Broughton, deceased. (p. 201)

CLEVELAND, James
　　3 March 1783. 12 Sept. 1791.
　　Wife: Frances Cleveland. Children: Johnston, Hannah and George Cleveland.
　　Exrs: wife, son Johnston, brother Alexander Cleveland, Benjamin Mason.
　　Wit: F. Adams, Ann Adams, Susannah Humphries. (p. 202)

McGEATH, James
　　27 Aug. 1791. Inventory. (p. 203)

SHRIEVE, Benjamin
　　30 Dec. 1790. September Court, 1791.
　　Wife: Anne Shrieve. Sons: William, Benjamin, Joshua and Abner Shrieve.
　　Daughters: Mary Mead, Elizabeth Moffett, Grand children: Robert, Benjamin,
　　and Nancy Moffett. Exrs: sons William, Benjamin and Joshua Shrieve.
　　Wit: Thomas Fouch, Jonathan Fouch, Isaac Fouch, Jr. (p. 204)

PERFECTS, Christopher
　　16 Aug. 1791. 13 Dec. 1791.
　　Wife: Catherine Perfects. Sons: Robert, James. Dau: Elizabeth. Grand-
　　daughter: Nancy Roper. Exrs: wife and daughter Elizabeth Roper. Samuel
　　Murray, John Littlejohn. (p. 208) Name signed in German.

LANE, James
　　29 April 1790. 13 Oct. 1791.
　　Wife: Lydia Lane. Children: Aaron Lane, Keren Smith (hus. George Smith),
　　Jane Smith (hus. Withers Smith), Hardage Lane, Sarah Lane (widow of son
　　James), surviving children of daughter Betty Remey (was wife of Jacob Re-
　　mey), Anne Payne, son James (dec'd.). Rev. Richard Major. Exrs: Aaron,
　　William and Hardage Lane (sons). (p. 209)

GORE, Thomas
　　7 Jan. 1792. Inventory.

HALL, Jonathan
　　9 Jan. 1792. Inventory.

DAVIS, John
　　29 Nov. 1791. January Court, 1792.
　　Legatees: Baptist church of which I am a member; Jenkins and Thomas Davis,
　　sons of brother; children of sister, Mary and Margaret Davis; nephew Evan
　　Davis, living in South Carolina; Mary Toy, housekeeper. Exrs: David Tho-
　　mas and William Osborn. (p. 217)

SHEPHERD, John
　　13 Feb. 1792. Inventory. (p. 220)

ECHART, Adam
　　Estate. (p. 222)

DOWLING, Daniel
　　Estate. (p. 226)

CHILTON, John
　　9 Aug. 1786. Feb. 1792. Inventory.

DONOHOE, Margaret
　　Account. 1792.

HUGELEY, Abraham
　　2 July 1792. September Court, 1792.

Sons: Charles and George Hugeley. Daughters: Polly, Margaret Summers (?) and her children, Polly and George, Cathy Tethern (?), Hannah Tebit, John Tebit and Hannah Tebit (stepchildren). Wit: Peter Frean, M. Rooney, Jacob Hugeley. (This will is almost illegible) (p. 250)

KIMBLARS, John [Kimblar]
17 June 1792. 10 Sept. 1792.
Wife mentioned, not named. Children: John, Sarah, other children mentioned. Exr: son John. Wit: Thomas Aden, James McKim, Alexander McKim. (p. 251)

HUFFMAN, John
20 March 1792. Sept. 1792.
Wife: Margaret Huffman. Sons: Henry, Peter and Philip. Wit: Peter Harman and others, names in German. (p. 252)

GREGG, Thomas
21st Day of 5th Month, 1792. September 1792.
Wife: Mary Gregg. Sons: Thomas, Joseph, Isaac, --- (illegible), Samuel, Levy. Daughters: Mary and Dinah Gregg. Exrs: son John and William Gregg (son). (This will is almost illegible)

TURLEY, Sarah
20 Sept. 1791. Sept. 1792.
Exrs: sons Ignatus and John Turley. Wit: John Veale, Thomas Veale and Lydia Veale. (p. 256)

THOMPSON, Andrew
8th Day of February, 1791. ---.
Wife: Penelope Thompson. Sons: Lomax, Isaac and Andrew Thompson. Exrs: wife and son Lomax. Wit: Adam Vincill, Jeremiah Prudane, Jacob Wincill.

MOXLEY, Joseph
4 Sept. 1792. Oct. 1792.
Wife: Margaret Moxley. Legatees: Cornelius Connelly (son-in-law), Penny Neal (gr. dau.), grandson Roaham (Rodham) Neal, Margaret Connelly (gr. dau.). Exrs: sons Joseph and Samuel Moxley. Wit: William Moxley, Thomas Moss, Joshua Danniel. (p. 268)

CLEWS, Joseph
15 Aug. 1792. Oct. Court, 1792.
"Beloved wife" but does not name. Sons: Thomas and Joseph Clews. Daughters: Mary, Elizabeth, Anna, Nancy, Ruth, Phebe. Gr. dau: Nancy Lovett (dau. of Jonathan Lovett). Wit: John Fairhurst, Joseph Gore. (p. 271)

ROZZELL, Stephens
10 Oct. 1792. 20 Oct. 1792.
Wife: Sarah. Children: Stephen, Sally, Phebe and Nancy. Exrs: son Stephen, Jonathan (?) George, S. Triplett. Wit: John Vanhorn, Jonah Queen, --- Hains. (p. 283)

CAVIN, John
27 Nov. 1787. January Court, 1793.
Wife: Mary (?) Cavin. Sons: Joseph and William Cavin. Grandsons: John and William Cavin (sons of Robert Cavin). Legatees: Elener Wilson (alias Nixon) and brothers James and Alex Wilson. Granddaughter Elizabeth Wilson. Sister Elizabeth Burton. Exr: son William Cavin. (p. 297)

SMITH, Clator
22 July 1792. 11 Feb. 1793.
Wife: Winnifred (?) Smith. Sons: Nathaniel, Clator, Charles, Conner and S---. Daughters: Elizabeth Hamten, Nancy, Jemima Ticha. Brother: George. Wit: William Cockerille, Mary Hoppoch, William Littler. (p. 301)

TODDS, Robert
18 Feb. 1793. ---.

Wife: Mary Todds. Sons: Robert, Samuel, John, Samuel. Grand daughter: Rebekkah Todds. Exrs: wife and son Robert. Wit: Abraham Cavin, John Hamilton, William Roberts. (p. 308)

MEYERS, George
    19 July 1791. April Court, 1793.
    Wife: Mary Barbara Meyers. Mentions children of first wife – does not name. Exrs: wife and son-in-law George Schwink. (p. 309)

VEALE, William
    4 Sept. 1792. May 1793.
    Wife: Lydia Veale. Children: John, William, Thomas, Amos, Charles, Sarah, Susannah, Lucas, Peggy and Polly Veale. Exrs: wife and son Charles.

CALDWELL, Joseph
    22 May 1792. Sept. Court, 1793.
    Children: Moses and Jean Caldwell. Exr: son Moses. Wit: Timothy Nixon, William Cavin, David Phillips.

BREWER, Henry
    5 May 1789. Sept. Court, 1793.
    Legatees: daughter Rebecca and her husband Daniel Sanford, grandson Henry Sanford; daughter Elizabeth Miner (Minor) and husband Nicholas Miner; grand children, John and Elizabeth Sanford. Exr: son John Brewer.

EBLENS, Jane
    30 July 1793. 9 Sept. 1793.
    Legatees: William Marshall (brother), nephews James and Samuel Marshall (sons of brother Joseph Marshall); Joseph Gore (son of John Gore); sister Mary N---, sister Elizabeth McConley. Exrs: Samuel Marshall, Joseph Gore.

JANNEY, Joseph
    3rd Month, 1789. October Court, 1793.
    Mentions wife, does not name. Sons: John, Thomas, Joseph Janney. Daughters: Sarah, Elizabeth, Hannah, Rebecca, Susannah and Mary. Exr: son John. Wit: Mahlon Janney, James Moore, A. Moore. (p. 341)

BROWN, Thomas
    16 Oct. 1791. Sept. Court. 1793.
    Sons: Joseph and Coleman Brown. Daughters: Betty (hus. John Lewis); Rebecca (hus. Joseph Aubrey). Grandchildren: Rebecca Lewis and Richard Brown (son of Joseph Brown). Exrs: son Coleman Brown, Jeremiah Cockerille.

BOOK "E"

THOMAS, John
    15 Sept. 1791. 9 Dec. 1793.
    Wife: Catherine Thomas. Legatees: Thomas Blinstone, Sarah Semple, William Blinstone (called William McCabe) – these were children of wife. Children of John Thomas – Leonard Taylor Thomas, Martha Jackson, Mary Hole, Joseph Thomas – to last three, a shilling each. Exrs: wife and son Leonard T. Thomas. Wit: Charles Binnis and Simon Binnis. (p. 1)

FIELD, Jamima
    10 Oct. 1791. 13 Jan. 1794.
    Daughter: Eleanor Reed. Grandson: Samuel Priest. Exr: Albert Russell (friend). Wit: A. Russell, Mary Huey, Melea Russell. (p. 5)

HELMS, Meredith
    13 Jan. 1794. Estate account.
    With Josias Herbert and Mary Littleton (late Mary Helms). (p. 5)

CAVINS, John
        Inventory. Appraisal of estate 10 Feb. 1794. (p. 8)

MAHUE, James
        21 July 1793. 10 Feb. 1794.
        Wife: Izable. Son: Moses Mahue. Wit: William M. Offutt, Peter Lamy,
        Elihu Harden. (p. 9)

McKNIGHT, William
        10 Feb. 1794. Inventory.
        Apprs: Owen Thomas, John Warford, Richard Thatcher.

HALLING, John Wilcoxen
        Feb. 1794. Division of estate. (p. 15)

FIELD, Jemima
        14 April 1794. Inventory. (p. 18)

BROWN, Thomas
        14 April 1794. Inventory.

HOWELL, Timothy
        5th Day of 2nd Month, 1794. 14 April 1794.
        Wife is mentioned but not named. Daughters: Deborah, Phebe, Elizabeth
        Meredith, Jane Poole and Ann. Sons: Samuel, Mahlon, Thomas Howell.
        Grandson: Henry Nickols. Exrs: John Gregg, Richard Thatcher. Wit: James
        Dillons, William Smith, Israel Janney. (p. 22) (Quakers)

LANE, James
        15 April 1794. Appraisal of estate.
        Apprs: Amos Fox, D. Talbott, Walter Bayne.

FOX, William
        27 July 1793. 15 April 1794. Inventory.
        William Littleton, George Kilgore, John Bowan Ryon. (p. 30)

CLEVELAND, Frances
        12 Dec. 1793. 15 April 1794.
        Daughter Hannah Coleman and granddaughter Frances Coleman. Sons: George
        and Johnson Cleveland. Mentions land on the "Western Waters." Exrs: son
        Johnson and Benjamin Mason. Wit: Jeremiah Hutchison, Benjamin Thomas
        and Susannah Humphries. (p. 32)

TODD, Robert.
        12 May 1794. Inventory. (p. 33)

GRIGGS, George
        23rd Day of 5th Month, 1772. 10 March 1794.
        Wife: Elizabeth Griggs. Daughters: Hannah, Mary, Sarah, Elizabeth and
        Ruth. Sons: William (eldest), Elias, to have a tract of land over the moun-
        tain, George to have a tract of land when twenty-one years of age. Exrs:
        wife and son William. Wit: Frances Hague, Isaac Hague, Thomas Hague and
        Abel Janney. (p. 35)

SWINDLER, Henry
        April 1794. Estate Account. (p. 38)

LEASE, John
        24 April 1794. 12 May 1795.
        Wife Catherine Lease, extrix. Brother George Lease. Legatees: Dortha
        Betzer and Hannah Kailer (sisters). Wit: John Parrott, Barbara Kailer, Han-
        nah Kailer.

GREGG, Levi
        12 May 1794. Inventory.

Apprs: Edward Conrad, John Pancoast, Robert McCullah.

NICKOLLS, Henry
14 March 1794. 12 May 1794.
Children mentioned, not named. Exrs: wife Susannah and Isaac Nickolls.
Wit: Stacy Taylor, Joshua Hatcher, Constantine Hughes. (p. 41)

HANSON, Gustavous
23 Feb. 1794. April 1794.
Wife: Sarah Hanson. Mentions four daughters, but does not name. Wit: Robert Thomas and Charles Lewis. (p. 43)

HALL, Richard
April 1794. Inventory.
Apprs: Benjamin Edwards, Godfrey Kiphard, Peter Harbert. (p. 44)

THOMPKINS, James
24 April 1794. 12 May 1794.
Children under twenty-one years of age. Extrx: wife Massa (?) Thompkins.
Wit: John Littlejohn, John Campbell, Aaron Daily. (p. 46)

SCOTT, Robert.
July Court, 1794. Inventory. (p. 48)

BROWN, Thomas
23rd Day of 4th Month, 1794. 14 July 1794.
Wife: Ann Brown. Sons: Moses and Aaron. Daughters: Rachel, Leah, Tamar and unborn child. Exrs: wife Ann, Benjamin Mead, Jonathan Lovett. Wit: James Trahern, Mahlon Baldwin, John Whitacre. (p. 48)

BROWN, William
13 Nov. 1788. 14 July 1794.
Wife mentioned, not named. Sons: Richard, William, John, Jacob Brown. Daughters: Hannah Schooley, Elizabeth, Sarah. Exrs: sons Richard and William.

MINOR, Spencer
April 1794. Inventory. Apprs: John Parrott, Edward Carter.

THOMAS, Catherine
4 Aug. 1794. Sept. Court, 1794.
Sons: Thomas Darrell, John Darrell, William Blinston (called McCabe). Judgment against Henry McCabe to go to William Blinston. Susan and Catherine Semple, daughters of Sally Semple, dec'd. Exrs: John Brown, William Kiwan, James Semple. (p. 54) John Brown, George Brown and William Blinston (son).

TURNER, Fielding
10 March 1793. Sept. 1794.
Sons: Lewis Major, Fielding, John Turner and unborn child. Wife: Winnifred. Exrs: Jere. Hutchison, John Hawley, Charles Lewis. John Berkley, John Davis, James Dutton, John Hutchison. (p. 55)

POLING, Samuel
9 Sept. 1794. Inventory. Martin Poling, administrator.

WADE, Zephania
9 Sept. 1794. Inventory. (p. 57)

THOMAS, John
9 Sept. 1794. Inventory. (p. 58)

LANE, James (Maj.)
13 Oct. 1794. Inventory of estate. William Lane, Jr.
Apprs: H. Stewart, Charles Eskridge, Francis Adams.

FOX, William
13 Oct. 1794. Inventory.

NOLAND, Philip
15 March 1794. 5 Sept. 1794.
Sons: Awbrey, Thomas Noland and grandson Thomas Noland (son of Philip),
each to receive five shillings. Daughters: Elizabeth Luckett, Molly Ann Luckett (hus. John), and her son Philip Luckett to have land in Frederick Co.,
Md. Wit: Jacob Myers, James Elliott, Ann Williams. (p. 67)

FOUCH, Isaac
25 March 1793. 13 Oct. 1794.
Wife: Mary Fouch. Sons: Thomas, Jonathan, George, Daniel, Isaac and William. Daughters: Mary, Elizabeth Russell and grand daughter Mary McDowell Russell (dau. of Elizabeth Russell). Exrs: sons Thomas, Jonathan,
George Fouch. Wit: George Elgin, William Elgin, Gustavous Elgin. (p. 69)

SOUTHARD, William
15 Nov. 1784. Nov. 1794. Inventory. (p. 72)

POWER, Joseph
21 Aug. 1794. 8 Dec. 1794.
Wife: Sarah Power. Exrs: son Walter Power. Wit: Samuel Canby, Mary
Fitzsimmons, Elizabeth Luke. (p. 74)

JOHNSTON, George (Dr.)
Oct. 1794. Account. Executor: Leven Powell.

COCKE, William
30 April 1794. 13 Oct. 1794. (p. 79)
Estate to be divided into two parts. Son Washington Cocke and daughter Lucy
Cocke. Wit: Leven Powell, Thomas Taylor, Josias Weeden, Chandler Peyton.

BRADEN, Robert
24 Aug. 1794. 12 Jan. 1795.
Children: Joseph Braden (lives in New Jersey), Robert Braden, Margaret
Wright. Exrs: son Joseph Braden and Robert Wright. Wit: Bartleson Fox,
Christian Climor. (p. 83)

MUSGROVE, William
Jan. Court, 1795. Inventory. Administrator: Nathan Smith.

COWGILL, Ralph
9 Nov. 1794. 9 Feb. 1795.
Wife: Sarah Cowgill. Children: Isaac, Hannah, Tamer, Dorothy, James, Joseph, Ralph. Exrs: sons James and Ralph. Wit: Robert Wynn, Robert Russell, William Carter. (p. 85)

THOMPSON, Israel
11th Day of 1st Month, 1795.
Wife: Sarah Thompson. Mentions land near Goose Creek Meeting House -
this land was bequeathed to him by his father at decease of sister Prudence
Woodward. Daughters: Nancy, Betsy, Sally and Prudence. Joseph Ritchardson, son of first wife. Mentions land in Kentucky. Exrs: sons Isaac, Jonah
and Samuel Thompson. Burr Powell appointed attorney. Wit: Mahlon Janney,
Benjamin Purdain, John Redman. Attached to the above will is a contract between Israel Thompson and Sarah Hague whereby she agrees to accept the sum
of 600 pounds in case he dies first. Date of 20 May 1778. Witnessed by Ann
Sheane. (p. 87)

MULL, David
4 Dec. 1794. 14 April 1795.
Wife: Margaret Mull. Children: George, Rachel, Madlain, David. Wit:
George Mull and Jeremiah Purdune. (Signed in German) (p. 93)

CARR, John
30 Oct. 1788. 10 Feb. 1795.
Sons: Thomas, John Carr. Grandsons: Joseph Carr (son of Peter), John Carr, William Carr (son of Peter), Daniel Carr (son of daughter Sally). Son-in-law Robert Wade. Exrs: Peter Carr and Joseph Braden. Wit: John Vanpelt, Robert Braden, Jr., Elizabeth Braden. (p. 96)

SKINNER, Phenas.
5 Nov. 1794. April 1795. Inventory. (p. 97)

JACKSON, William
5th Day of 2nd Month, 1782. 14 April 1795.
Wife: Abigail Jackson. Daughters: Martha Sheeld, Mary Shale, Sarah, Ann and Febe. Sons: John, James and Richard Jackson. Exrs: wife Abigail. Wit: Benjamin Purdum, Elijah Houghton. (p. 104)

OXLEY, Rachel
April 1795. Estate account. Administrator: James Stevens.

HAWKINS, John
14 April 1795. Inventory. (p. 106)

JACKSON, William
14 April 1795. Inventory. (p. 107)

SMARR, John
9 June 1794. 8 June 1795.
Wife: Sarah Smarr. Sons: Perit, Andrew, George, Charles, Samuel, Reuben, John, Robert Smarr. Daughters: Elizabeth Smarr, Ann Smarr, Mary Hampton, Jane Weaden, Sarah Tilman, Fanny Smarr, Cloe Moore, Nancy Williamson. Exrs: Wife, Robert Smarr. Wit: William Gallenher, David Gallenher and William Powell. (p. 109)

TURNER, Fielding
13 July 1795. Inventory. (p. 116)

MASON, Benjamin
1 Nov. 1791. 13 July 1795.
Wife Ann Mason, to stay with the family for one year then should she choose to leave is to have ten pounds currency. Sons: George, Burgess, John, William Woolverton Mason. Daughters: Ann Linton, Margaret Carter, Elizabeth Gist, Caty Linton, Mary Mason and Margaret Mason. Exrs: son William W. Mason. Wit: Jeremiah Hutchinson, Charles Dunkin, William Beaty, Edward Edwards. (p. 116)

PAGIT, Francis
7 May 1790. July Court, 1795.
Wife: Ruth Pagit. Sons: Timothy, Reuben Pagit. Daughters: Rachel Cunningham, Elizabeth Wohund, Mary Lewis, Nancy Hillfine, Peggy Evens, Sinthy Miller, Frances and Amy Pagit. Exrs: son Timothy and Thomas Lains. Wit: William Eskridge, James Hutchinson, Joshua Hardy, Jacob James. (p. 120)

LANHAM, Aaron
28 May 1792. 8 April 1795. A codicil added 8 April 1795.
From Montgomery, Md. Sons: Walter, Hezekiah, Ladock, Aquilla, land in Md. Daughters: Elizabeth, Lethe, Mercy Ann, Eleanor. Exr: son Walter Lanham. (p. 121)

CONRAD, Jonathan
1 June 1795. 14 Sept. 1795. (p. 130)
Wife: Guulme Conrad. Mentions three "little daughters." Exrs: Joseph Beale, Edward Conrad. Wit: John Gregg, Nicholas Osborne, Bazella Miller.

HAIDEN, Charles
14 Sept. 1796. Inventory. (p. 133)

CAMPBELL, James
    20 Jan. 1795. 4 Sept. 1795.
    Legatees: brothers Andrew, Robert and John Campbell, father William Camp-
    bell. Exrs: brother Andrew Campbell. Wit: George A. Lewis, John West, Mar-
    garet James.

PANCOAST, Israel
    12 Oct. 1795. Inventory.

DULY, Charity
    19 Oct. 1795. Inventory.

KING, Benjamin
    7 Aug. 1794. 4 April 1795. (p. 146)
    Sons: John (land in Fairfax Co.), William (land in Prince William Co.), Dan-
    iel (land in Prince William Co.), Benjamin. Daughter: Susannah Williams
    (wife of John Williams). Granddaughter: Susannah Kent (dau. of John Kent).
    Exrs: sons Daniel, John and Benjamin King. Wit: Charles Brent, Nancy Selfe.

GREGG, Stephen
    2nd Day of 11th Month, 1795. 8 Feb. 1796.
    Wife: Susannah. Sons: Thomas, Nathan, Samuel Gregg. Daughter Susan.
    Exrs: sons Nathan and Samuel Gregg. Wit: Israel Janney, Jesse Janney,
    William Brown. (p. 165)

SMALLWOOD, Luke
    10 Feb. 1796. Estate Account. John Nickland, administrator.

HUMPHREYS, Thomas
    18 Jan. 1796. 14 March 1796.
    All estate to brothers and sisters, not named. Exrs: Thomas Humphreys
    (father) and Abner Humphreys (brother)

REED, R.
    19 Jan. 1795. 14 March 1796.
    Account - R. Reed to William Reed, administrator.

CAMPBELL, James
    24 Nov. 1795. Estate appraised. (p. 169)

CRUMBACKER, John
    1 Aug. 1795. 11 April 1796.
    Wife Eve to have estate until son John Crumbacker comes of age. Son Jacob
    and daughter Elizabeth - only children named. Exrs: wife Eve Crumbacker.
    Wit: Adam Shover (Shaver), Jacob Cost.

LOCKER, John
    12 April 1796. Sale account. (p. 173)

HALBERT, Michael
    No date. 11 April 1796.
    Wife: Rosey Halbert. Daughters: Sally Halbert, Polly Beavers. Children:
    Katy, William, Thomas, Michael, James, Lydia and Ailsy. Exrs: wife, Wil-
    liam Lane, Joshua Buckley. Wit: Ann Gold, Joseph Gold, Joseph Asbury.

HUMPHREYS, Thomas
    12 April 1796. Inventory. (p. 175)

TRAMELL, Sampson
    11 April 1796. Inventory.

ELLZEY, William
    29 July 1795. 12 April 1796. (p. 184)
    Legatees: Albert Russell and Ann, his wife; daughters: Lucy, Margaret, Sar-
    ah. Sons: William and Lewis. Exrs: "beloved wife" (not named) and son William.

POWELL, Elisha
    28 Feb. 1796. 9 May 1796.
    Sons: Robert, William, Elisha and John. Daughters: Mary Powell, now Mary
    Middleton, Sarah Powell, now Sarah Fulton. Exrs: sons William and Robert
    Powell. Wit: Charles Lewis, William Johnston, Enoch Triplett. (p. 190)

HEADEN, George
    12 Sept. 1796. Inventory.

THOMAS, David
    23 June 1796. 12 Sept. 1796.
    Legatees: Martha Thomas (daughter-in-law); daughter Sarah and her husband,
    George Evans, to have land in Westmoreland Co., Pa.; sons Philip and
    George. Exrs: Owen Thomas, Philip Thomas, George Thomas (all sons).
    Wit: Nathan Nickolls, George Nickolls, Timothy Taylor. (p. 200)

JENKINS, John
    23 July 1796. 12 Sept. 1796.
    Legatees: sister Elizabeth Self, Charles Jenkins (son of William). Exr: Pres-
    ley Self (nephew). Wit: Francis Moore, Sylvester Jenkins. (p. 202)

BROWN, Isaac
    5th Day of 5th Month, 1796. 12 Sept. 1796.
    Sons: Isaac, John, Abraham Brown. Daughter: Martha Whitacre. Exrs: son
    Isaac Brown and Edward Whitacre. Wit: James Burson, Jonathan Burson,
    John Burson. (p. 202)

COCKERILLE, Christopher
    10 Oct. 1796. Inventory. (p. 240)

HARLEY, Elizabeth
    26 Feb. 1796. 10 Oct. 1796.
    Legatees: John Gunnell and William Shreve (son of William Shreve, Mary-
    land). The suit of the administrator of John Harle should abate at the decease
    of Elizabeth Harle, suit to be renewed by her executors. Exrs: John Gunnell
    (of Loudoun Co.) and Henry Gunnell of Fairfax Co. Wit: William Stanhope,
    Henry Gunnell, Jr. and Charles Brent. (p. 212)

SKINNER, Phineas
    12 Oct. 1796. Account of estate. (p. 213)

HUTCHINSON, Benjamin
    15 Nov. 1796. Inventory.
    Apprs: John Hawley, Andrew Heath and Timothy Pagit. (p. 233)

CARR, Thomas
    7 Sept. 1796. 15 Nov. 1796.
    Wife: Mary Carr. Daughter: Jane Camell (Campbell ?), wife of Andrew.
    Sons: John, Thomas, James, Joseph, Samuel Carr. Daughters: Margaret
    Carr, Mary Hall, Elizabeth Carr. Exrs: sons Thomas and James Carr.
    Wit: J. Burns, Jr., William Mains, Levi Hale. (p. 234)

PHILIPS, Thomas
    15 Sept. 1794. November Court, 1796.
    Legatees: children of sister Sarah Martin, Israel Netson (or Nelson), Eliza-
    beth Martin, Thomas Martin. (p. 236)

BOGAR, Frederick
    8 Dec. 1796. Inventory.

GREEN, Thomas
    23 April 1788. December Court, 1796.
    Young children - William, Fielding and Frances Green. One shilling each to
    following legatees: Elihu Harding (son-in-law) and his children; daughters
    Ann, Elizabeth Shelton, Mary Bennett, Polly Sanders, Frances Green. Sons:

Thomas, George, Gerrard Green. Extrx: wife Frances Green. Wit: William Fox and J. R. Borbridge. (p. 237)

BROWN, Benjamin
4 Oct. 1795, 10 Oct. 1796.
Wife: Winnifred Brown. Legatees: Mary Fox (wife of William), Catherine, daughter of Mary Fox, James Owen, William Middleton. Exrs: James Owens, William Middleton. Wit: John West, William Stanhope, Mary Douglas. (p. 255)

BEALLY (Beatty.?), James
March Court, 1797. Inventory. (p. 277)

HUPPOCH, Elsey
29 Jan. 1797. 9 Feb. 1797.
Legatees: George ---, Elizabeth Crager, John, Peter and Cornelius Huppoch. Exr: Anthony Huffman. Wit: C. Stump, Jacob Stump. (p. 257)

EBLIN, John
13th Day of 8th Month, 1795. --- 1797.
Wife: Mary Eblin. Daughters: Eliza Parker, Hannah Carter, Mary Pyatt, Rachel Stone. Sons: John, Isaac and Samuel Eblin. Son-in-law Thomas Chapman. Exrs: James Carter (son-in-law) and Jonathan Lovell. (p. 258)

HOUGH, John
21st Day of 2nd Month, 1797. April 1797.
Sons: William, Samuel, Jonah, Mahlon and Amos, 1000 acres of "land in Monogahaley County." Grandsons: Samuel and Benjamin Hough (bros.). Grandchildren: Mary and Mahlon (sons of son John, dec'd.); dau. Sarah Mason (hus. Abraham). Exrs: sons William, Samuel and Mahlon.

LEWIS, Vincent
10 Nov. 1786. 10 April 1797.
Sons: John (eldest), George, Joseph, James and Charles (youngest). Daughters: Betty (wife of Jonathan Davis) and Anna Jennings. Exrs: wife Ann and son Charles. (p. 287)

WILLIAMS, Richard
20 March 1795. 8 May 1797.
Sons: Jenkins, Joseph, James and Enos - "to Enos all my land." Daughters: Mary Shrieve, Margaret. Grandson, William George. Wife mentioned. Exrs: son Enos and Charles Bennett. (p. 297)

MAJOR, Richard
2 Nov. 1796. 8 May 1797.
Wife: Sarah Major. Children: Elijah, James, Sarah Hutchison, Rebecca Beaver and children of deceased son, Daniel. Granddaughter: Elizabeth Major. Exrs: James Crooks, Jeremiah Hutchison, Sr. Wit: Joseph Mershon, Joshua Hutchins, Thomas Mershon. (p. 303)

SANDERS, John
7 April 1797. 29 April 1797.
Wife: Mary Sanders. Sons: James and John (under 21 years). Daughters: Sarah, Elizabeth, Barbary, Mary, Patience, Nancy, Bethany and two infants "not named yet." Exrs: wife, Pressley Sanders, Aaron Sanders (brothers)

CHICK, William
January Court, 1797. Inventory.

TAYLOR, Thomas
30 Jan. 1797. 10 July 1797.
Sons Henry and Joseph, to have land in Va. and Md. Children: Ann, Mary, Rachel, Sarah, Thomas and Jesse. Exrs: Thomas Taylor (son) and Benjamin Hough (son-in-law). (p. 317)

GRIGSBY, James
>19 June 1797. August Court 1797.
"All estate to Mary Reed (housekeeper) and the five children I have had by her." Children: Lewis Grigsby Reed, Ludwell Grigsby Reed, John Grigsby Reed, A -- G. Reed, Nathaniel Grigsby Reed. Exrs: Peter Stump, William Field. (p. 325)

HUGELEY, Charles, Sr.
>7 March 1797. Sept. 1797.
Wife: Mary Hugeley. Son George and other children. Exrs: sons John, Job, George Hugeley. (p. 227)

BOTTS, Joshua
>2 March 1797. 11 Sept. 1797.
Wife: Judith Botts. Son Moses. Daughter Elizabeth. Grandchildren, Hutson and Nancy Overfield. Son-in-law Martin and wife Elizabeth. Exrs: wife, son Moses. Wit: John Warford, George Lewis, James Grady. (p. 328)

REDMAN, John
>----. 11 Sept. 1797.
Mother: Mary Redman. Sister: Mary McKinley. Brother: Andrew Redman. Nephew: William McKinley. Exrs: brother Andrew Redman, Jonah Thompson (friend). Wit: John Nicklin, James Brown, Stephen Ball. (p. 330)

BOOK "F" 1797-1802

McGEATH, William
>10 Sept. 1798. Inventory.
Apprs: William Gregg, William Right (Wright), James Ball. (p. 1)

HOWELL, Timothy
>9 Nov. 1797. Inventory.
Apprs: Stacy Taylor, Abner Osborne, James Dillion. (p. 2)

ELLIS, Ellis
>1 May 1792. December Court, 1797.
Legatees: sister Hannah Davis and her son. Exrs: Abraham Davis (brother-in-law). Wit: Benjamin Huffty, Edward McGinnis, Jean McGinnis. (p. 8)

GRIGSBY, James
>12 Dec. 1797. Inventory.
Apprs: Nathaniel Smith, James Taylor, Jno. Cotton.

JANNEY, Elizabeth
>14th Day of 12th Month, 1797. 8 Jan. 1798. Nuncupative will.
All estate to daughter Cosmelia. Wit: Mahlon Janney, John Moore, James Moore.

LEWIS, James
>12 Jan. 1798. Inventory. Admr: Charles Lewis. (p. 15)

HIXON, William
>22 Dec. 1797. 12 Feb. 1798. Inventory.

CARR, John
>February 1798. Estate account. Peter Carr, administrator.

JENKINS, John
>12 March 1798. Estate appraised.

SMITH, Mary
>2 April 1798. 10 April 1798.
Children: Rachel Adams, Susannah Smith (daughter-in-law), Sally, Phillipina Fitchelharles (?), Ann Jacoby, Catherine Smith (dau.-in-law), Catherine Derry (or Durry), Sybilla, John. Exr: son-in-law Jacob Jacoby. Wit: Fred-

erick Smith, Martha Smithley (last name in German). (p. 2l)

McCABE, Henry
11 April 1798. Inventory. (p. 22)

GOLEY, Thomas
18 Dec. 1798. Inventory.
Apprs: Daniel Lewis, John Linton, Charles Lewis. (p. 33)

GRYMES, Nicholas
6 Jan. 1798. 14 May 1798. (p. 30)
Wife: Jain Grymes. Children: Nicholas, William, Silvester, John, Edward, Sanford, Sarah King, Alice Jenkins, Jain Grymes, Anna Grymes. Exrs: sons William, Silvester, Nicholas. Wit: George Payne, Charles Brent, Stephen Lay.

STEPHENS, James
8 July 1798. August Court, 1798.
Wife: Hannah Stevens. Sons: James, Hezekiah, Henry, George, William,
Benjamin and Zachariah. Daughters: Ann Fouch, Elizabeth Ward, Hannah
Brooks (hus. Aaron). Legatees: Reuben Stephens Homan, Hannah Homan,
Mary Homan, Mathew Homan, Mark Homan - children of Elizabeth Homan.
Exr: son Henry Stephens. Wit: Solomon Littleton, Jenkin Oxley, Hugh Lester.

FARROW, Joseph
23 April 1784. Estate account. (p. 38)

TITLETT, Samuel, Sr.
20 Aug. 1798. 10 Sept. 1798. (p. 40)
Sons: Giles, Samuel, Edward, James Titlett. Daughters: Mary Songster, Jane
Stone, Ann Bennett (and her children, Joseph, Polly, Patty, Sally, Duhannah,
Samuel Bennett), Sarah Hammitt, Margaret Barnett, Elizabeth. Exrs: sons
Giles and Samuel. Wit: Robert Perfect, Eramus Perfect, John Littlejohn.

WHITE, James
Oct. 1797. 10 Sept. 1798. Inventory.

COOPER, Frederick
10 Sept. 1798. Estate account. Jacob Shoemaker acting as executor of estate.

WIRTS, Peter
6 Jan. 1798. 10 Sept. 1798.
Wife: Christina. Sons: John, Michael, William, Jacob and Peter. Daughters:
Christina, Catherine and Anna Mary. Exr: son Michael Wirts.

FOWKES, Robert
1796. 10 Sept. 1798. Inventory.

ANSLEY, William
14 June 1798. 11 Sept. 1798.
Extrx: wife Ann Ansley. Slaves, Daniel and Joseph, to be free. Wit: William
Rhodes, George Rhodes, Joseph Ashton. (Written in German) (p. 49)

BARDEN, Thomas
1798. Inventory.
Apprs: James Marshall, Joseph Gardner, William Buchanan.

THOMAS, George
31 March 1787. 10 Oct. 1798. (p. 52)
Legatees: son William Thomas, sons-in-law Isaac Steer, John Steer and Joseph Steer (brothers), estate to be divided among the three. Exrs: Isaac
Steer, Joseph Steer and John Steer. Wit: Josias Clapham, Leonard Ansel.

FULTON, Robert
2 Jan. 1792. 10 Oct. 1798. (p. 55)
Sons: Robert, James, David, John. Daus: Lenah, Milly. Wife is mentioned

but not named. Exr: son Robert Fulton. Wit: John Bivins, Aaron Sanders.

SWART, John
    29 Aug. 1798. 8 Oct. 1798.
    Wife: Elizabeth Swart. "Estate to be divided among all my children" - not
    named. Exr: James Batson. Wit: Leven Powell, John Batson, Adrian Hagerman.

ADIN, Thomas
    18 Oct. 1798. Inventory.
    Apprs: James Lewis, Joseph Lewis and Vincent Davis. (p. 57)

TALBOTT, Joseph
    25th Day of 7th Month. 10 Dec. 1798. (p. 63)
    Wife: Rebekah Talbott. Children: Samuel, Joseph, Sarah, Mary, Elisha, Jesse,
    Ann, Elizabeth, Susannah, John and Rebekah. Exrs: James Ballikin, James
    Moore, Asa Moore. Wit: Richard Griffith, J. Williams, Israel Thompson.

HUGELEY, Charles
    12 Oct. 1797. 10 Dec. 1798. Inventory. (p. 68)

PINQUITE, Esther
    21st Day of 4th Month, 1791. Jan. 1799.
    Legatees: Agnes, Nance and Joanna Davis; Sarah Matton [Madden ?] and her
    sister Mary; Ambrose, Ann and Mary Martin (children of Israel Matton);
    Bernard Taylor; children of John and Jain Pinquite; children of Samuel and
    Agnes Nance. Exrs: Bernard Taylor, Ambrose Taylor and David Davis.
    Wit: Jonathan Taylor, William Taylor, Margaret Patterson. (p. 71)

MYERS, Christopher
    15 Feb. 1798. Inventory. (p. 72)

LANE, James
    1799. Inventory.

HICKMAN, Conrad
    June 1799. Inventory.

FINE, Peter
    1798. 8 Dec. 1799. Feb. 1799. (p. 83)
    "Ill in health and body." Wife: Catherine Fine. Legatees: Elizabeth Sinken, child
    of my dau. that I raised. Children mentioned, not named. Exrs: Isaac Ritchey.

COWGILL, James
    24 Jan. 1799. Feb. 1799. (p. 88)
    Legatees: mother, brothers and sisters - not named. Exrs: Ralph Cowgill
    and Samuel Mosley. Wit: Robert Wyman, William Carter, Robert Russell.

McPHERSON, Stephen
    2nd Day of 2nd Month, 1799. 14 Oct. 1799. (p. 122)
    "Aged and stricken in years." Wife: Ann McPherson. Sons: John, Stephen,
    Joseph, Daniel, William, Jesse. Daughters: Rachel Boyer, Ruth Meville (?).

HAINS, Thomas
    22 July 1799. 14 Oct. 1799.
    Children: Hephyidah, William, Stacy, Thomas and Simeon. Daughters: Sarah
    and Mary. Mentions land in Pa. Extrx: wife Mary. Wit: Joseph Braden,
    Obed Pierpont and John Eblin. (p. 122)

FEARST, Christian
    9 Oct. 1799. 13 Jan. 1800.
    Wife Hannah Fearst and children. Wit: Andrew Copeland, John Campbell,
    John Blair, Robert White. (p. 132)

DANIEL, William
27th Day of 8th Month, 1799. 4 April 1800.
Wife: Esther Daniel. Children: James, Daniel, Sarah Lewis, William, Jane Cadwallader, Esther Richards, Martha Rhodes, Joseph, Benjamin, Rachel Sinclair and Samuel and Samuel Daniel. Granddaughter: Alice Smith. Exrs: wife, sons Joseph, Benjamin, Samuel. Wit: Stacy Taylor, John Head, William Evans.

INDEX OF BOOK "F"

Anderson, John
Ansley, Henry
Areel (?), Richard
Aubrey, Francis
Aubrey (Awbrey), Henry
Aubrey, John (Heirs of)
Aubrey, Samuel
Aubrey, Thomas

Ball, John
Benson, Charles
Benson, Mercer
Berkley, Burgess
    (Heirs of)
Booth, John
Booth, John
Braisler [Brewster?],
    Thomas (dec'd.)
Brown, Henry
Brown, William
Bryan, Thomas
Buckley, William
Buckner, Peyton (dec'd.)

Caldwell, Hugh
Campbell, Eneas (Enos)
Carr, John
Carroll, David
Chambers, William
Clapham, Josias
Clary, Benjamin
Claypool, Joseph
Clewes, Thomas
Colclough, widow
Coleman, Richard
Connell, Thomas
Cox, Harmon
Cox, Harmon
Cox, John
Crutcher, James
Crutcher, Judwin

Davis, David
Dixon, John
Dixon, Joist
Dormon, Hanson
Dunbarr, George

Elgin, Francis (of Cocke)
Elliott, Will
Eskridge, Charles
Evan, Will
Evans, Mary

Fairhurst, Jeremiah
Fan, Jacob
Fouch, Isaac (of Cocke)

Garner, Silvester
Garrett, Edward,
    Executors
Gore (?) (Goard), Joshua

(of Cocke)
Gore, Thomas
Gregg, George
Gregg, George (of Cocke)
Gregg, John
Gregg, Michael
Gregg, Samuel
Gregg, Thomas
Griffith, George

Hague, Francis
Hague, Francis
Hague, John
Hall, William, Jr.
Hambey, Will (Executors)
Hambrey [Sambrey] -
    Executor
Hamby (Hambey), John
Hamilton, James
Harle, John (Executors)
Harris, Samuel
Harris, William
Harrys, David
Hatcher, James
Hatcher, John
Hatchner, William
Heryford, John
Hollins, William
Hollins, William
Hopkins, John
Hough, John
Hutchinson, Benjamin
Hutchinson, Daniel
Hutchinson, Jere
Hutchinson, John
Hutchinson, Joseph

Jackson, Lovell,
    executors
Janney, Abel, Sr.
Janney, Ann
Janney, Jacob
Janney, Jacob B.
Janney, Joseph (of Abel)
Janney, Mahlon
John, Thomas

Keen, John
King, William
Kirk, William
Kirkbridge, Manlon

Lane, James
Laswell, Jacob
Lewis, John, Sr.
Lewis, Thomas
Lewis, Vincent
Lindsay, Abraham

Massey, Lee
McDowell, James
McGeach, Joseph

Mead, John
Mead, William
Middleton, John
Minor, Nicholas, Col.
Moore, Henry
Morton, Edward
Morton, Thomas
Moss, John
Murray, James (?)

Neal - administrator
Nickols, Isaac
Nickols, Thomas
Noddy, William
Noland, Peter
Noland, Philip
Norton, Edward

Osborne, John
Osborne, Nicholas
Owens, William
Owsley, John
Owsley, Pine
Owsley, Thomas
Owsley, William

Peyton, Craven
Peyton, Francis
Philips, James
Poole, Benjamin
Potts, David
Potts, Jonas
Potts, Jonathan
Potts, Samuel

Read, Joseph, Executor
Remey, Jacob
Rhoades, Moses
Roach, Richard
Roberts, Richard
Russell, Anthony
Russell, Samuel

Sands, Edward
Self, Thomas
Shreve, Benjamin
Shrieve, Benjamin
Simmonds, Thomas
Sinclair, John
Sinclair, Margaret
Smith, Jacob
Stone, Samuel
Stone, Thomas
Stump, Thomas
Summers, Grant, Sr.

Thompson, Israel
Trammell, John
Trammell, William
Turner, Fielding
Turner, William
Tyler, Charles

Walker, Isaac
West, William, Capt.
Wilkes, Francis

Wilkes, John
Williams, Walker
Williams, Will

Winsor, Thomas
Winsor, William, Executor
Wiseheart, Henry

MILITIA OF LOUDOUN COUNTY

Adams, Francis, Ensign
Alexander, John, Captain
Alexander, John, Lt. Colonel
Bageley (Bagley), John, 1st Lt.,
   15 May 1781
Ball, Farling, Captain, 13 May 1777
Beaty, Thomas, 2nd Lt., 12 Feb. 1781
Bennett, Charles, Captain, 9 Oct. 1780
Berry, Withers, Ensign, 11 June 1781
Brooks, Vincent, Ensign, 9 Sept. 1777
Burnes, Joseph, Captain, 11 Feb. 1783
Callett [Catlett], Alexander, 2nd Lt.,
   Sept. 1777
Cavens, William, Ensign, 10 March 1778
Cavens, Williams, Captain, 11 Aug. 1779
Cleveland, James, Captain, 8 Nov. 1779
Coleman, James, Major, 13 Jan. 1777
Coleman, James, Colonel, 14 Nov. 1780
Debell, John, 2nd Lt., 12 July 1780
Debell, William, 2nd Lt., 12 June 1780
Debell, William, 1st Lt., 12 Feb. 1781
Dehaven, Abraham, 1st Lt., 14 May 1781
Dehaven, Isaac, Ensign, 14 May 1781
Dodd, William, Ensign, 10 March 1778
Douglas, Hugh, Ensign, 10 March 1778
Douglas, Hugh, 1st Lt., 13 March 1781
Douglas, Hugh, Captain, 14 May 1781
Douglas, William, Captain, 13 May 1777
Elgin, Francis, Jr., Ensign, 10 May 1779
Eskridge, Charles, Major, 9 Sept. 1777
Furr, (Enoch), 1st Lt., 11 June 1781
George, William, Captain, 11 Feb. 1782
Gilbert, Silas, Ensign, 9 Dec. 1782
Hancock, Simon, Captain, 9 Sept. 177-
Hixson, Timothy, Captain, 11 Feb. 1782
Hopkins, David, Ensign, 9 Oct. 1780
Hough, Joseph, Ensign, 13 March 1781
Hutchison, William, Ensign, 12 July 1779
Kernans, Thomas, 2nd Lt., 9 Sept. 1777
Kilgore, George, 1st Lt. 14 June 1779
King, Herman (?), 2nd Lt., 10 March 1778
King, Smith, 2nd Lt., 10 April 1781
King, Thomas, 1st Lt., 14 May 1781
King, Thomas, Capt., 9 Dec. 1782
Lane, William, Sr., Captain, Oct. 1777
Lewis, Daniel, 2nd Lt., 10 March 1778
Lewis, Thomas, Captain, 13 May 1777
Linton, John, Captain, 12 Feb. 1781

Littleton, John, Ensign, Sept. 1781
Marks, Elisha, Ensign, 9 March 1778
Marks, Elisha, Captain, 9 Oct. 1778
Mason, William, 1st Lt., 8 Dec. 1782
Mason, William T., Ensign, 14 May 1781
McIllhaney, James, Major, 14 Nov. 1780
McIllhaney, James, Captain, 14 May 1781
McIllhaney, James, Captain, 11 March 1782
McLean, John, Ensign, 12 Feb. 1781
Mellan, Thomas, Ensign, 8 Nov. 1779
Minor, Michael, Jr., Ensign, 9 Oct. 1780
Minor, Thomas, Ensign, 12 Feb. 1781
Moss, John, Captain, 13 June 1777
Niles, Josias, Ensign, 13 May 1777
Niles, Josias, 1st Lt., 10 March 1776
Oliphant, Samuel, Ensign, 9 Oct. 1780
Ousley, William, 1st Lt., 9 Sept. 1777
Payne, Henry, 1st Lt., 9 Sept. 1777
Reed, Jacob, Major, 12 Feb. 1781
Repess, Thomas, Captain, 13 Jan. 1781
Repess, Thomas, Major, 14 May 1781
Repess, Thomas, Lt. Col., 11 March 1782
Russell, Robert, 2nd Lt., 11 June 1781
Rust, George, 2nd Lt., 9 Oct. 1780
Sanders, Gunnell, Lt., 13 Jan. 1777
Sanders, John, Ensign, 13 Jan. 1777
Shores, Thomas, Captain, 12 Feb. 1781
Sinclair, John, Lt., 13 May 1777
Slemmer, Christian, Captain, 11 Aug. 1799
Smiths, Withers, 2nd Lt., 12 June 1780
Summers, George, Captain, 9 June 1777
Taylor, John, 1st Lt., 12 Feb. 1781
Taylor, William, Major, 13 March 1781
Thomas, Enoch, 2nd Lt., 14 May 1781
Trammill, Sampson, Captain, 10 April 1781
Triplett, Simon, Colonel, 12 Feb. 1781
Ury, Spencer, 1st Lt., 10 April 1781
Vandevanter, Isaac, 2nd Lt.,
   10 March 1778
Vince, Thomas, Ensign, 14 May 1781
West, George, Captain, 13 May 1777
West, George, Lt. Col., 14 Nov. 1780
West, George, Colonel, March 1782
Whaley, James, 2nd Lt., 10 March 1778
White, Joel, Ensign, 12 June 1780
White, Joel, 2nd Lt., 12 Feb. 1781
Wildman, Joseph, 2nd Lt., 10 May 1779

The above persons were recommended for the Militia of Loudoun Co., Va. (Copied from Minute and Record Books on file in county clerk's office, Leesburg, Va. From Book "G".)

FAMILIES OF SOLDIERS IN THE CONTINENTAL ARMY
Ordered provided for on the date given. Loudoun County, Virginia.

Broken, George, widow, 14 April 1778
Brown, John A., wife Sarah Brown, 12 May 1778
Butler, Robert, wife Mary Butler, 5 Sept. 1777
Coleman, Joel, wife Jamima Coleman, 9 Aug. 1779
Coleman, Joseph, widow, 14 April 1778
Collen, Joseph, widow, 14 April 1778
Columbus, John, 14 April 1778
Cummings, William, son in the army, wife Bridget Cummings, 10 March 1778
Farnsworth, John, widow of, 14 April 1778
Gilmore, William, son in army, wife Elizabeth, 10 Nov. 1778
Hamilton, David, wife Jane Hamilton, 11 Aug. 1777
Harris, Henry, wife Sophia, 12 May 1778
Henderson, Adam, widow Catherine, 12 Sept. 1780
Henderson, Hugh, wife, 8 Feb. 1779
Hill, Richard, wife Margaret, 9 March 1778
Howell, John, wife, 9 Feb. 1779
King, Richard, wife, 12 May 1778
Lassure, Andrew, wife, 14 Dec. 1778
Lovett, William, wife, 14 April 1778
Pinkstone, Shadrack, wife, 10 March 1778
Reeder, Shadrack, wife Elizabeth, 10 March 1778
Rhodes, Jacob, children to be furnished, 10 Nov. 1778
Rhodes, Mary, husband in the army, 10 Nov. 1778
Rice, James, widow Hannah Rice, 9 Oct. 1780
Richards, Thomas, wife Ann Richards, 9 Oct. 1780
Rinker, Edward, 14 April, 1778
Russell, Samuel, wife Sarah Russell, 13 Nov. 1780
Sharks, Conrad, son in army, 9 Aug. 1779
Slact, Covert, in 18 month draft, 10 Dec. 1781
Spencer, James, an aged person who has four sons in Cont'l. Army, 15 April 1777
Spitz, Benjamin (name Spitfathen), son in army, 12 May 1778
Stokes, John, wife, 11 Feb. 1777
Tritepoe, Conrad, wife Mary, 15 May 1781
Welch, Elizabeth, husband in army, 9 Nov. 1778
Wilcox, Eleanor, a soldier's wife, 11 Feb. 1782

PENSIONS
Date placed on pension and age

Alder, George, Maryland, 1818, 62
Carney, William, Virginia, 16 Sept. 1818 (Dec'd. 3.3.1818), 70
Elmere, John, Virginia, 4 Sept. 1818, 86
Fry, Nicholas, Maryland, 4 March 1820, 87
Goff, Adam, Virginia, 12 Aug. 1818 (d. 2.18.1825), 69
Hilliard, John, Virginia, 1818, 80
Near, John, Pennsylvania, 1818, 95
Oram, Henry, Virginia, 1818, 76
Powell, Leven, Virginia, 1825, 71
Quick, John, Virginia, 26 Jan. 1824 (dec'd. 16 June 1831), 98
Russell, John, Virginia, 1825, 78
Welles, Nathaniel, Virginia, 1818 (d. 27 July 1832), 75

COMMENCEMENT OF PENSIONS - 1831

Begeant, William, Cavalry, Va. Cont'l., 29 May 1833, 79
Brown, Isacher, Private, Va. Militia, 28 Feb. 1833, 73
Butler, Jacob, Private, Va. Militia, 23 April 1833 (d. 9 June 1833), 76
Coombs, John, Private, Va. Militia, 26 March 1834, 80
Copeland, James, Cavalry, Va. Militia, 28 Feb. 1833, 75

Dailey, Jesse, Private, Va. Militia, 1 Nov. 1832, 73
Davis, James, Fifer, Va. Cont'l., 28 Feb. 1833, 73
Elgin, Walter, Pr. & Sgt., Va. Militia, 25 Feb. 1833, 78
Francis, Thomas, Private, Va. Cont'l., 26 March 1834, 75
Gideon, Peter, Private, Va. Militia, 22 May 1833, 82
Griffith, Thomas, Private, Va. Militia, 28 Feb. 1833, 77
Harvin, Edward, Private cav., Va. Militia, 17 April 1834, 77
Hixon, James, Private cav., Va. Militia, 20 April 1834, 71
Hogeland, James, Private, Va. Militia, 28 Feb. 1833, 74
Hough, Bernard, Private, Va. Cont'l., 28 Feb. 1833, 71
Iden, John, Private, Va. Militia, 28 May 1833, 82
Kline, John N., Private, Pennsylvania, 28 Feb. 1833, 73
Lee, Ludwell, Private, Va. Militia, 16 May 1833, 73
Long, Jacob, Private, Va. Militia, 19 Dec. 1832, 73
Mount, Ezekiel, Private, Va. Militia, 17 Jan. 1833, 76
Munday, Aaron, Private, Va. Militia, 10 April 1833, 72
Munroe, Spencer, Private, Va. Militia, 27 Feb. 1833, 74
Selden, William C., Surgeion, Va. St. Troops, 30 June 1832
Stoneberger, John, Private, Va. Militia, 17 May 1833, 72
Wade, Robert, Private, Va. Militia, 11 Jan. 1832, 73
West, John, Artificer, Va. Militia, 26 Oct. 1833, 80
Wigginton, Benjamin, Va Militia, 18 March 1834, 71
Wornell, James, Pr. & Sgt., Va. Militia, 11 Sept. 1833, 70

DEED BOOK "1"
Grantor, date, and grantee

Abrell, John, 10 Oct. 1757, P. (Peter) Noland
Barker, Joseph, 13 Sept. 1757, Catesby Cock (Fairfax Co.)
Berkeley, John, 4 March 1758, Charles Tyler
Carlile, John (lease), 16 Nov. 1757, John Dalton, Fairfax Co.
Davis, Richard (Of Culpeper Co.), (lease), 7 Nov. 1757, David Davis
Fox, George W., 17 July 1757, Isaac Hollingsworth (Of Frederick Co.)
Hatcher, William, 30 Aug. 1757, Isaac Nickolls
Hollingsworth, Isaac (Of Frederick Co., Va.) (lease), 28 Aug. 1757, John Norman
    (Loudoun)
Hutchison, Andrew, 6 Aug. 1757, John & Daniel Hutchison (sons)
Janney, --, 14 March 1758, Janney --- (Deed of gift)
Janney, Abell, 14 March 1758, Joseph Janney
Janney, Mahlon, 13 March 1758, James Hamilton
John, Thomas, 7 March 1758, Jacob Reed
Mead, Samuel, 8 Nov. 1757, William Mead & Jno. Poultney
Minor, Nicholas, 13 Feb. 1758, Israel Thompson
Minor, Nicholas, 13 Feb. 1758, John Morse
Minor, Nicholas, 17 Feb. 1758, Michael Stoker
Minor, Nicholas, 4 March 1758, Benjamin Edwards
Minor, Nicholas, 14 March 1758, James Abbott
Minor, Nicholas, 14 March 1758, Mahlon Janney
Minor, Nicholas, 14 March 1758, John Hough
Noland, Philip, 9 Aug. 1757, John Welles (lease)
Noland, Philip, 30 Sept. 1757, Joshua Pyburn (lease)
Noland, Philip, 30 Sept. 1757, John Peters - late of Maryland
Robert, Richard, 14 March 1758, Thomas Green
Rust, Peter, Gent. Of Westmoreland Co., Va., 18 July 1757, John Ariss-Westmoreland
Rust, Peter, Gent., 19 July 1757, John Ariss
Shreve, William, 29 Oct. 1757, Rec. 14 March 1758, David Carrill
Shreve, William, 29 Oct. 1757, Rec. 14 March 1758, David Carrill
Stukesberry, Robert, 1 July 1757, Jacob Janney
Stukesberry, Robert, Sr., 8 Oct. 1757, Thomas Gore
Sutherland, Alexander - Cf Loudoun Co., 25 Aug. 1758, Catesby Cocke - of Fairfax Co.
West, George, bond as surveyor - 9 Aug. 1757

Ball, Charles Dr. / born Dec. 14, 1793 / died 1823 /
Ball, Isabella Garham / dau. of Dr. Charles B. Ball/ b. Jan. 20, 1819 / died July 1, 1837 /
Ball, Lucy / wife of Dr. Charles Ball / born Jan. 13, 1793 / died June 27, 1870 /
Brown, Fielding / born April 21, 1826 / died Jan. 11, 1870 /
Caldwell, Augusta, born 1838 / died 1857 /
Caldwell, Elizabeth / born Jan. 8, 1792 / died March 29, 1866 /
Caldwell, Mary Elizabeth / consort of S. B. T. Caldwell / died 1850 / aged 46 years.
Carr -- (son) / died 1835 / 4 years of age /
Carr, Priscilla / died Dec. 21, 1831 / 76 years of age /
Carr, Virginia Ellen / died 1838 / 4 years of age /
Clarke, Addison / b. July 10, 1791 / died 1874 / 63 years of age /
Clarke, Isaac Vandevanter / son of Addison and Mary Clarke / b. March 30, 1845 /
    died 1865 / A Confederate Soldier /
Clarke, Mary / wife of Addison Clarke / born 1805 / died 15 Jan. 1877 /
Coleman, Ann Mary / died 1827 / age 19 years / wife of Edmund Coleman /
Coleman, Edmund / died 1836 / 30 years of age /
Coleman, Infant / of Edmund and Mary Coleman / died 1827 /
Coleman, William / died Dec. 8, 1828 / aged 53 years /
Connor, John / died Sept. 26, 1842 / 37 years of age /
Connor, John Isaac / son of John & Lucinda / died 1842 / 4 years of age /
Cooksey, John / born 1820 / died 1893 / aged 73 years /
Cramwell, Susan / died 1856 / aged 64 years / "Sacred to Memory of our Mother" /
    (On Caldwell lot)
Downs, James / died March 12 / 1849 / aged 25 years /
Dresh, Eleanor / died / 1836 / 62 years of age / (date is either 1836 or 1856)
Dykes, Anna / died Feb. 28 / 1844 (or 1841) / age 80 years /
Elgin, Charles / died 1824 / 55 years of age /
Elgin, Francis / died 1851 / age 26 years /
Fauntleroy, Charles M. Col. / son of Gen. T. T. Fauntleroy & wife Anne Magill /
    born Aug. 21, 1822 / died July 28 / 1889 /
Fauntleroy, Janet / wife of Col. Charles M. / died Sept. 5 / 1849 / aged 27 years /
Fitchet, Naomi / died 1842 / 80 years of age /
Gardner, Mary E. / daughter of Catherine Gardner / b. 28 May / 1824 / d. 1878 /
Garner, Catherine / died Dec. 12 / 1886 / aged 86 years /
Garner, James / died 1849 / aged 64 years of age /
Garner, Margaret / wife of James / died 1885 /
Gore, Rowena / born Oct. 8 / 1795 / died 1856
Hall, Eliza Ann / died July 5 / 1865 / 54 years of age /
Hall, Mary / died 1853 / 84 years of age /
Hall, William / b. 1810 / died Oct. 20 / 1890 /
Hawling, Elizabeth / d. 25 Aug. / 1862 / aged 84 years /
Hawling, John / son of John & Hannah / died 1847 / aged 66 Years /
Hawling, Mary / daughter of John & Hannah / died 1832 / aged 56 years /
Howard, John / died 1836 / 49 years of age /
Humphrey, Jane / died 1827 / aged 92 years /
Hunt, Lewis / d. 1876 / 92 years of age /
Kitzmiller, Elizabeth / wife of Martin / b. Jan. 31 / 1778 / d. March 12 / 1843 /
Kitzmiller, Martin / born 13 April / 1772 / died Mary 24 / 1826 /
Knox, Catherine / wife of Thomas / died 1855 / aged 58 years /
Knox, Thomas / died Feb. 21 / 1871 / aged 76 years /
Lacey, Charles H. / b. August 8, 1826 / died 1905 /
Lickey, Mary / wife of George / daughter of E. & Ellen Retan (?) / d. 1858 / age 21/
Mains, Mary / consort of William / died 1827 / age of 85 years /
Mains, Washington / died 1813 / 31 years of age /
Mains, William / illegible /
McDonough, James / died June 5 / 1842 / 75 years of age /
Nixon, George / b. March 12, 1789 / died Sept. 30 / 1876 /
Nixon, Joel Lewis / no inscription
Nixon, Mary Jane / no inscription
Norris, Ann / no dates

Norris, Ignatus / no dates
Norris, Mary / no dates
Peers, A----n / died Sept. / 1832 / age 36 years /
Potter, Ebenezer / died 1807 / age of 40 years /
Potter, Elizabeth / died Feb. 1844 / age of 75 years / (other stones illegible)
Pyley, Joseph Willis / died 1847 / 18 years of age /
Rice, Elizabeth / wife of David / dau. of Ezra & Ellen Rolow (?) / died Aug. 1875 /
        21 years of age /
Rice, Jesse / died 1826 / 43 years of age /
Rice, Thirza / widow of Jesse / b. Oct. 23 / 1789 / d. Nov. 12 / 1853 / 64 years /
Shipley / infant son of John Shipley / died 1848 /
Shipley, Ann / b. 1798 / died -- / 43 years of age /
Simpson, Elizabeth / b. 28 Jan. 1811 / died June 24 / 1876 /
Slaymaker, Addison Clarke / son of Amos & Lizzie / b. 1858 / d. 1863 /
Slaymaker, Julia / died --- / age 46 years /
Slaymaker, Lizzie / wife of Amos / b. 1839 / died 18 March / 1875 /
Smart, Lucybel / died 1843 /(buried on Wherry lot)
Sterrett, Samuel / b. 20 August /1797 / d. June 9, 1834 /
Tebbs, Mary / dau. of A.S. & J.E. Tebbs / died 1849 /
Tebbs, William / son of A.S. & J.E. / died 1857 /
Thomas, James / died 1882 / aged 83 years /
Thomas, Martha / wife of James Thomas / b. Aug. 10 / 1804 / d. 1863 /
Thrift, ---- / died April 10 / 1861 / 62 years of age /
Thrift, William / died April 30, 1852 / 72 years of age /
Trayhern, Sallie / wife of James Trayhern / b. 1826 / died 1852 / (On Caldwell lot)
Vandevanter / small grave with M.E.V.
Vandevanter --- / wife Of -- Carr / illegible
Vandevanter, Ann / wife of Isaac / died 1845 / age of 35 years / (On Mains lot)
Vandevanter, Caroline / consort of Isaac / Vandevanter / 1812 / died 1841 /
Vandevanter, Elizabeth / wife of Joseph / died 1834 / aged 59 years /
Vandevanter, Flavins Braden / son of Gabriel and Mary / d. 1838 / 3 years /
Vandevanter, Isaac / died 1834 / 60 years of age / (On Mains lot)
Vandevanter, Joseph / died 1824 / 46 years of age /
Vandevanter, Mary / died 1846 / aged 79 years /
Vandevanter, Mary Elizabeth / wife of Gabriel / died 1836 / 27 years of age /
Vandevanter, Mary Elizabeth / dau. of Isaac / died 1838 / age 17 years /
Virts, John Henry / 1846 / 1860 /
Wherry, Elizabeth / --- /
Wherry, Mary E. / wife of John Smart / died 1847 / (illegible) /
Wherry, Silas / (illegible) /
Williams, James / b. 180(6) - D. 18(36) (?) /

Old Methodist Cemetery

Ainsley, William / died 1798 / aged 42 years /
Cross, James / b. 1767 / died 1830 /
Cross, Nancy / wife of James Cross / b. 1769 d. --- /
Delahand, John / b. 1740 / d. 1831 /
Dorram (?), Mary Ann / wife of Thomas / died 1849 / 52 years of age /
Gilmore, Elizabeth / died 1848 / aged 32 (or 52) years of age /
Head, Mary / mother of George Head / b. 1758 / died 1823 / ---- /
Hillard, Ann Eliza / second wife / of Joseph Hillard / died 1852 /
Hillard, Sophia / consort of Joseph Hillard / died 1825 /
Morallee, Sarah / died 1843 / 65 years of age /
Morallee (?), Sophia / died 1845 / 58 years /
Morallee, Thomas / died 1829 / age 53 years /
Rose, Anna / wife of Col. George Rose / b. 1772 /
Rose, John (Captain) / b. Sept. 3, 1761 / died Feb. 4 / 1844 /
Russell, Benjamin / died 6 Oct. 1836 / 51 years of age /
Shaw, John / born 1776 / died --- /
Tilton, Daniel / b. 1767 / died 1830 /

Note: This cemetery is near the Episcopal church - most of the stones have fallen or
been removed to make way for a tennis court.

Benedict, Henrietta Gray / born 1814 / died 1890 /
Benedict, William B. / born 1811 / died 1852 /
Claggett, Lalla, wife of Dr. Thomas Claggett / dau. of John & H.B. Gray / born /
    1820 / died 1888 /
Claggett, Thomas, Dr. / (no date of birth) / died Oct. 18 / 1870 /
Dawson, Samuel / (inscription illegible) /
Dawson, Sarah / (illegible) /
Douglas, Ann / wife of Charles Douglas / died Feb. 20 1866 / 66 years of age /
Douglas, Charles / died 1872 / age --- (?) /
Douglas, Hugh / died 1815 / 56 years of age /
Douglas, Louisa Ann / dau. of Hugh and Catherine Douglas / died 1817 / 16 years /
Douglas, Margaret / died August 20, 1826 / 58 years of age /
Gray, Henrietta / wife of John / died 1861 / 42 years of age /
Gray, Isabella / b. Sept. 1822 / died 1863 /
Gray, John / died 1844 / 61 years of age /
Gray, Rebecca / 17 June 1812 / 1883 /
Harrison, A --- Blackburn / born 1838 / died 1879 /
Harrison, Anne Maria / dau. of William Burr Harrison & wife Sarah Powell / born /
    7 Dec. 1829 / died 1908 /
Harrison, Burr W. / born 1798 / died --- (illegible) /
Harrison, Edward Burr / son of W.B. and Sally Harrison / born 1827 / d. 1852 /
Harrison, Elizabeth Conrad / dau. of William Burr and Sarah P. Harrison / born
    1836 / died 1907 /
Harrison, Sally / wife of W. Burr Harrison / died 6 Oct. 1845 / 46 years of age /
Heaslip, Isabelle / died Dec. 1820 / aged 73 years /
Lee, George Dr. / born Blanfield / Essex Co. Va. / died at Leesburgh, Va. / born
    Jan. 20, 1801 / died 1858 /
Lee, Maria / (illegible) /
Mason, Sally Inness / wife of Steven Mason / dau. of Murray Forres (?), of Fal-
    mouth / born July 31, 1824 / died Aug. 30, 1843 /
Mason, William T. / died 1862 / ---- --- /
McIllhany, Elizabeth (child's grave)
McIllhany, James / --- (grave of a child)
McIllhany, Margaret / wife of James McIllhany / dau. of Edward & Ora Henderson /
    died 1844 / 39 years of age /
Moore, Ann Mason / wife of Thompson W. Moore / died 1855 (no date of age) /
Moore, Westwood Thompson / died 1826 / ---- --- /
Noland, Catherine / died 26 April / 1849 / age 94 years / (an adjoining grave -
    inscription illegible)
Reed (Reid), Frances / died Feb. 22 / 1823 / 76 years of age /

(This old cemetery in a state of neglect)

City Cemetery, Leesburg

Abbott, Mary E. / b. 1838 / d. 1908 /
Abbott, Sarah / 1834 / 1898 /
Aldridge, John / died 1895 / 80 years of age /
Aldridge, Mary E. / died 1876 /
Aldridge, Robert / son of John and Mary Aldridge / killed at Mt. Lookout / 1861 /
    19 years of age /
Aldridge, Rose / died 1885 / aged 22 years /
Allison, Julia / died 1910 / age of 65 years / (Letcher lot)
Arnold, James T. / son of John and Sarah / died 1893 / drowned /
Arnold, John / born -- 1826 / d. 1900 /
Arthur, Annette Allen / only daughter of Harvey / born 1896 / d. 1907 /
Arthur, Katherine Lee / wife of Harvey / b. 1857 / died 1900 /
Ball, Henry Whitmore / son of George & Annie W. Ball / b. 1882 / d. 1899 /
Ball, William / b. 1812 / d. 1891 /
Beales, Rodney / d. 1919 / age of 85 years /
Beard, Ella / wife of Lewis Beard / b. 1816 / d. 1879 /
Beard, Lewis / b. 1802 / 1868 /

Benjamin, William / b. 1841 / died 1933 (?) / (See Funkhouser)
Bennett, Carrie Quarles / dau. of E. L. and R. H. Bennett / 1879 / 1901 /
Bennett, Edward L. / b. 1842 / d. 1901 /
Bennett, Frank Leon / son of R. H. Bennett / b. 1877 / died 19--- /
Bennett, Robert Edward Lee / son of E. L. & R. H. Bennett / 1877 / 1897 /
Bennett, Ruth / b. 1851 / 1906 /
Bitzer, John / 1847 / 1916 /
Bradshaw, Margaret / 1834 / 1899 /
Brecenridge, Susan / b. 1839 / died 1924 / 85 years of age /
Breckenridge, Alexander / 1832 / died 1916 /
Briscoe, Eliza Harris / wife of William Briscoe / b. 1797 / (on lot William Harris
    and Hannah Moore)
Burch, Mary Virginia / wife of Edgar Burch / b. 1850 / d. 1889 /
Chancellor, Elizabeth Mildred / wife of Samuel / 1822 / 1897 /
Chancellor, Helen Ellzey / 1850 / 1921 /
Chancellor, Rush Wallace Dr. / 1849 / 1897 /
Chancellor, Samuel Ashley / 1821 / 1839 /
Chichester, Ann Thompson / died 1817 / 47 years of age / dau. of Thompson Mason /
    of Raspberry Plantation / and his wife Mary K. Barnes /
Chichester, Arthur Mason / Capt. C. S. A. / son of George Mason Chichester and /
    Mary Bowie / died 1916 / aged 65 years /
Claggett, Haddie (Gray) / wife of Thomas H. Claggett / b. Feb. 23, 1842 / died1911 /
Claggett, Thomas / died 1881 / aged 42 years /
Clarke, Eugenia / wife of Frank Fred / died 1897 / in Oklahoma Territory /
Cockerill, Lucy / dau. of Richard & Anne (Coleman) Cockerille / died 1919 / aged
    84 years /
Coleman, Edmond / son of Edmond Coleman & wife Caroline Wilson / died 1879 /
    44 yrs. /
Conner, Ada Mountjoy / wife of Davidson Conner / 1857 / 1931 /
Conner, Davidson / 1848 / 1911 /
Crawford - See Tebbs
Crockford, Hattie / dau. of S. J. & H. S. Tebbs / died 1874 / 27 years of age /
    (See Tebbs)
Dade, Lee M. / 1845 / 1918 / (Sanders lot)
Dade, Medora / wife of Lee M. Dade / 1844 / 1913 / (Sanders lot)
Dade, Mary R. / 1876 / 1897 / (Sanders lot)
Drake, Francis / b. March 5, 1797 / died 1897 /
Drake, Mary Ann / wife of Francis Drake / b. 1793 / died 1866 (1856) /
Dulin, Alfred / b. 1802 / d. 1881 /
Dulin, Elizabeth / 1849 / 1924 /
Dulin, Elizabeth Ann / dau. of Alfred Dulin / 1838 / d. 1926 /
Dulin, George Cephas / 1845 / 1928 /
Dulin, Margaret / b. 1812 /1889 /
Dulin, Nancy / consort of Edwin Dulin / died 1851 / 64 years of age /
Dunn, Minnie / wife of John Dunn / died 1915 / aged 47 years /
Elmore, Genevie Mitchell / 1869 / 1907
Everts, Charles / died 1905 / age 53 years /
Everts, Mollie / 1861 / 1891 /
Fairfax, Infant daughter / of Henry & Eugenia / d. 1898 /
Fairfax, Infant son of Henry & Eugenia / d. 1901 /
Fairfax, Henry / 1850 / d. 1916 / Eugenia Tennant, wife of Henry Fairfax /
Fairfax, John Walter / son of Henry & Elizabeth Fairfax /b. 1829 / Dumfries, Va. /
    died 1908 /
Fairfax, Lindsay / b. 1857 / d. 1917 /
Fishburne - see Claggett
Frederick, Annie P. / wife of Frank L. Frederick / dau. of G. D. & M. L. Smith /
    d. 1883 /
Freeman, Anna / died 1876 / --- --
Frye, Frederick / 1889 / 1929 /
Funkhouser, Frank / 1870 / d. 1900 /
Funkhouser, Mary Benjamin, wife of Frank Funkhouser / 1872 / 1903 /
Gibson, Susan / b. Sept. 1799 / d. Jan. 25 / 1844 /
Gidding, William / died 1886 / 39 years of age /
Gidding, William / son James & Susan Gidding / b. Cornwall, Eng. / 1821 / d. 1904 /
Hammond, Ellen Roberta / dau. of William & A. E. Gidding / d. 1901 / aged 50 years /

Handley, John J. / 1835 / 1907 /
Handley, Sarah / 1845 / 1923 /
Hanvey (Hanbey?), James D. / 1817 / 1867 /
Harper, Mary Amelia / wife of Robert Harper / 1828 / 1870 /
Harper, Robert / 1825 / d. 1908 /
Harris, Eliza / wife of William Briscoe Harris / b. 1797 / -- /
Harris, Richard Lee / 1852 / 1917 /
Harris, Sarah / 1854 / 1925 /
Harris, William B. / b. 1801 / 1888 /
Hartsel, Robert / 1860 / 19-- /
Havener, Virginia / wife of W. D. / died 1886 / age 84 years /
Havener, W. D. / died 1865 / 61 years of age /
Hawling, J. Lewis / 1816 / 1884 /
Hawling, Martha / wife of J. Lewis Hawling / 1821 / 1895 /
Heater, Richard / 1838 / 1918 /
Helm, Rev. Joseph / b. 1805 / d. 1890 /
Helm, Louis / died 1893 / aged 57 years /
Helm, Mary / wife of Rev. Joseph Helm / b. 1811 / d. 1896 /
Helm, Mary Clarke / b. 1829 / died 1902 /
Hendrick, Roberta Leckie / no dates
Higgins, Dennie / 1869 / 1908 /
Higgins, Mary Catherine / 1871 / 1930 /
Hogan, James / 1899 (died) / 46 years of age /
Inzer, George / 1836 / d. 1895 /
Jackson, Benjamin / "In Memory of son of William & Rebecca Jackson / killed at
        Gettysburg / 1863" /
Jackson, Charles F. / died 1829 / (another grave on lot - illegible)
Jackson, Elizabeth Clapham / b. 1839 / d. 1901 /
Jackson, George / 1855 / 1931 /
Jackson, Henry / 1852 / 1917 /
Jackson, Rebecca T. / wife of William / d. 1868 / 58 years of age /
Jackson, Samuel Clapham / 1835 / 1920 /
Jackson, William / 1808 / d. 1896 /
James, Charles E. / b. 1826 / d. 1909 /
James, Dora Esther / wife of Ernest James / 1818 / 1907 /
James, Sarah / wife of Charles E. James / 1828 / 1893 /
Janney, Alice / wife of John Janney / b. 1800 / d. 1881 /
Janney, Charles Philip / 1839 / 1925 /
Janney, John / b. 1798 / d. 1872 /
Jones, John / son of Richard and Catherine Jones / 1832 / 1910 /
Kelley, Charles / b. 1890 / d. 1914 /
Kelley, Hattie E. / 1860 / 1931 /
Kephart - "In memory of our father, b. 1795 / d. 1868." (Not named)
Kephart - "In Memory of our Mother / b. Dec. 11, 1811 / died 1867" /
Kephart, Barbara / died 1856 / 56 (or 63) years of age /
Kephart, Barbara / died 1856 / (same as above)
Kephart, Eugenia / 1833 / 1916 /
Kephart, Marion / son of George & Margaret Kephart / b. 1836 / d. 1888 /
King, Micajah Watkins / 1862 / 1914 /
Kirkpatrick, John Thomas / 1870 / 1931 /
Kirkpatrick, Marvin / 1894 / 1924 /
Kirkpatrick, Mary Della / 1873 / 1932 /
Laycock, John William / 1831 / 1902 /
Laycock, Lawerence / son of Adin & Margaret M. / 1889 / 1893 /
Laycock, Margaret Morton / wife of Adin / 1866 / 1893 /
Laycock, Mary / wife of John B. / 1836 / 1899 /
Lee, Nannie / dau. of Rev. A. D. and Elizabeth Lee / 1842 / 1908 /
Letcher, Ann Eliza Moffett / wife of Charles Letcher / b. 1838 / 1912 /
Letcher, Charles / 1836 / 1898 /
Littleton, Edgar / son of Thomas & Elizabeth / 1839 / 1874 /
Littleton, Elizabeth Buffington / wife of Thomas / b. 2 May 1802 / 1877 /
Littleton, Emma / b. 1826 / 1878 /
Littleton, F. B. / son of Thomas & Elizabeth / d. 1862 /
Littleton, Thomas / 1802 / 1886 /
Littleton, Virginia / dau. of Thomas & Elizabeth / 1838 / 1912 /

Long, Ada White / wife of Isaac Long / b. 1871 / 1907 /
Lott, Mary Smalle / wife of Parkinson Lott / 1809 / 1889 /
Major, Hannah / b. 1822 / 1893 / (on Harris lot)
Marlow, Anna Fox / wife of Edward Marlow / 1842 / 1910 /
Marlow, Edward / 1833 / 1905 /
Matile, E. Albert / 1898 / 1900 /
Matile, Flora / dau. of James / 1868. 1902 /
McNealey, Mary / d. Nov. 5, 1899 / 90 years of age /
McPherson, Lucy / wife of Mathew McPherson / 1823 / 1907 /
McPherson, Mathew / b. 1829 / 1908 /
Mercer, George Stuart / b. Belmont, Va. / 1867 / d. 1917 /
Mercer, Lee Washington / b. 1839 / d. 1915 /
Mercer, Martha E. / wife of E.W. / d. 1843 / 1897 /
Milner, Gertrude Ball / wife of Percy Milner / 1866 / 1918 (or 1913) /
Minor, America Spencer / wife of James / 1845 / 1920 /
Moffett, Paul / husband of Beulah / 1875 / 1928 /
Moffett, Thomas / died 1896 / aged 53 years /
Moffett, Vylinda H. Rush / wife of Thomas Moffett / 1847 / 1925 /
Myers, George E. / b. March 24 / 1838 / d. 1912 /
Myers, George W. / b. 1866 / d. 1929 /
Myers, Mary V. / wife of George W. / b. Sept. 20 / 1866 / ---- /
Myers, Sarah E. / wife of George E. / b. Nov. 15, 1843 / d. Aug. 1908 /
Newton, Charles A. / 1844 / 1916 /
Newton, Francis / 1826 / 1864 /
Newton, Sarah Wallace Hunter / wife of Charles A. Newton / 1847 / 1914 /
Nixon, Eliza / 1814 / 1897 /
Nixon, Florence / dau. of Joel & Mary Jane Nixon / died 1938 /
Nixon, J.L. / died 1891 / 70 years of age /
Nixon, Joel / b. 1818 / 1839 /
Nixon, Joseph Westwood / son of Levi & Margaret / 1853 / 1879 /
Nixon, Rev. L.B. / 1811 / 1875 /
Nixon, Levi / 1823 / 1889 /
Oden, Alexander / April 15, 1830 / 1905 /
Oden, Henry / 1863 / 1904 /
Orange, James / d. 1878 / aged 65 years /
Orange, Susannah / 1800 / 1877 /
Osborn, Emily / wife of Joab / 1820 / 1888 /
Osborn, Flavius / son of J. & E. / killed at Bull Run / (Osborn - Osburn)
Osborn, Joab / 1805 / 1890 /
Pancoast, Jane A. / wife of Joseph / 1832 / 1909 /
Pancoast, Joseph / 1827 / 1866 /
Peacock, Henry / 1823 / 1897 /
Peacock, Mary / b. in Ireland / d. 1898 / age 70 years /
Pleasants, Sallie / dau. of Robert and Bentley Pleasants / 1875 / 1906 /
Powell, Cordelia / wife of Edward Burr Powell / dau. of Henry & Christiana /
      Armstrong / b. 9 March, 1829 / July 1907 /
Powell, Elizabeth Burr / 1822 / 1897 /
Powell, Hugh Lee / b. 1839 / d. 1910 /
Powell, Lewellyn / son of Edward B. Powell / b. Dec. 11, 1858 / 1880 /
Powell, Mary Lowden / wife of Hugh L. Powell / 1863 / 1914 /
Powell, Mary Susan / 1835 / 1865 / (on same lot is grave of Susanna Gibson)
Rittenhouse, Benjamin Franklin / Major of U.S. Marines / 1869 / 1931 /
Roger, Mary / 1868 / 1905 / (Claggett Lot)
Rogers, Alec / eldest grandson of Dr. T.H. Claggett / d. 1893 / 32 years /
      (Claggett Lot)
Roxbury, M.W. / dau. of Francis & M.W. Drake / 1836 / 1919 / (Drake Lot)
Sanders, Beverly / died 1879 / aged 32 years /
Sanders, Wilson / 1811 / 1885 /
Seeder / 1854 / 1916 /
Seeder, George / 1829 / 1856 /
Shawen, Ann / wife of William C. / 1826 / 1888 /
Shawen, Cornelius / 1877 / 1916 /
Shawen, Harriett / dau. of W.C. & A.C. / 1849 / 1919 /
Shawen, Mary / dau. of William C. / 1858 / 1925 /
Shawen, Mary V. / wife of Cornelius / 1852 / 1911 /

Shawen, William / 1852 / 1917 /
Shawen, William C. / 1820 / 1880 /
Shoemaker, Amanda / 1823 / 1905 /
Shray, G.A. / b. 1851 /
Shray, J.H. / b. 1846 / --- /
Smith - three graves on this lot.
Smith, Ann Virginia / wife of William / 1830 / 1879 /
Smith, Annie / dau. of above / 1861 / 1868 /
Smith Clarence W. / 1871 / 1904 /
Smith, Edgar Dr. / son of George and Martha / 1842 / 1874 /
Smith, Jefferson / 1863 / 1923 /
Smith, Martha L. / 1814 / 1871 /
Smith, Rhoda F. / 1828 / 1907 /
Smith, William / 1819 / 1889 /
Smith, William H. / 1807 / 1896 /
Smith, William N.R. / 1858 / 1882 /
Sothern, Christiana / wife of William / --- /
Sothern, Christiana / dau. of William & Christiana /
Sothern, William / no dates
Spindle, Priscilla / wife of R.L. / 1840 / 1909 / (on Bradshaw)
Steadman, John W. / 1863 / --- /
Steadman, Lillian / 1870 / 1933 /
Stephens, John A. / died 1872 /
Stephens, Roxanna / wife of John / died 1895 / age 79 years /
Stocks, John / 1852 / 1915 /
Tebbs, Ann Cleveland / only dau. of Charles / and Fanny Tebbs / b. 1856 / 1879 /
Tebbs, William, Capt. / killed 1864 / 37 years of age /
Tittman, Otto Hilgard / b. Bell ville, Ill. / Aug. 20, 1850 / d. Aug. 20, 1938 /
Vandevanter, Washington / 1813 / 1900 /
Van Devanter, Cecelia / 1853 / 36 years of age /
Van Devanter, Charles G. / 1849 / 1933 /
Van Devanter, Mary E. / 1843 / 1864 /
Van Devanter, Virginia Kilgore / wife of Charles / 1847 / 1878 /
Westwood, George H. / 1929 / age 55 years /
Westwood, W. / died 1900 /
White -- Children of Col. E.V. White & wife Mary Elizabeth - Mary Elizabeth,
         Stephen, Melvin, Richard and Mary Elizabeth.
White, Mary Elizabeth / wife of Col. E.V. White / 1836 / 1893 /
White, Rosa Lee / 1865 / 1896 /
Wildman, Robert / 1849 / 1934 /
Wilkins, James / d. 1889 / 42 years of age /
Williams, America Spencer / wife of James / b. 1845 / d. 1920 /
Williams, James / 1841 / 1910 /
Williams, John / 1807 / 1874 /
Williams, Pleasants H. / wife of John / 1814 / 1893 /
Willoughby, Mary / dau. of Capt. W.W. & Mary Tebbs / d. 1897 (or 1895) /
Woodward, Annie / wife of John / b. 1829 / died 1915 /
Woodward, Newton / died 1931 / 75 years of age /
Wynkoor, Linnie A. / 1841 / 1898 /

Benedict, Henrietta Gray 61
    William B. 61
Benhams, John 20
    Robert 20
Benjamin, William 62
Bennett, Ann 51
    Carrie Quaries 62
    Charles 49
    Charles, Captain 56
    Duhannah 51
    E. L. 62 (2)
    Edward L. 62
    Frank Leon 62
    Joseph 51
    Mary 48
    Patty 51
    Phebe 33
    Polly 51
    R. H. 62 (3)
    Robert Edward Lee 62
    Ruth 62
    Sally 51
    Samuel 51
Benson, Charles 55
    Mercer 55
Berkeley, Catherine 35
    Elizabeth 21
    George 35
    John 58
    Reuben 35
    Scarlett 11
    Susannah 35
Berkly, William 28
Berkley, Ann 35
    Benjamin 35
    Burgess 35, 55
    Catherine 35
    Elizabeth 10
    Fanna Rogers 35
    John 44
    Nancy 35
    Reuben 27
    Scarlett 24, 27
    William 35
Berley, Moses 35
Berry, Withers, Ensign 56
Best, John 25 (2)
Betzer, Cortha 43
Beyland, David 26
Binnis, Charles 42
    Simon 42
Binns, Charles 29, 53
    Charles, Jr. 35
    John 29
Bishop, John 29
    Mary 29
Bist, James 8
    John 8
    Martha 8
    Rachel 8
    Thomas 8
Bitzer, John 62
Bivins, John 52
Blackburne, Richard 36
Blair, John 52
Bland, Robert 15
Blands, Robert 2
Blinston, William 44
Blinstone, Thomas 42
    William 42
Bodine, Jacob 8, 27
    John 36
Bogges, Henry 31
    Vincent 53
Boone, Hannah 37
Booth, James 1
    John 1, 55 (2)
    Robert 1

Borbridge, J. R. 49
Botts, Aaron 4, 26
    Archibald 39
    Elizabeth 50
    Joshua 50
    Judith 50
    Margaret 39
    Moses 39, 50
    Sarah 39
    Sebacah 4
    Seth 4
Boulton, David 7, 14
    Margaret 7
Bowers, Barnett 29
Bowie, Mary 62
Boyd, Betty 18
    J. 53
    James 18
    Jane 18
    John 26
    Nancy 18
    Samuel 53
    Thomas 18
    William 18, 20
    Williams 22
Boydston, Benjamin 18
    Mary 18
Boyer, Rachel 52
Boyers, George 29
Braden, Elizabeth 46
    Joseph 25, 27, 39, 45, 46, 52
    Robert 45
    Robert, Jr. 46
Bradfield, Hannah 33
Bradshaw, --- 65
    Margaret 62
Braisler, Thomas 55
Branner, Philip 28
Brasfield, Jacob 32
Brecenridge, Susan 62
Breckell, Elizabeth 14
    Wright 14
Breckenridge, Alexander 62
Brent, Caty 32
    Charles 47, 48, 51
    George 32, 53
    Hannah 19
    Hugh 32
    Martin 32
    Sarah 32
    Thomas 32
    Willis 32
Brewer, Henry 1 (2), 21, 42
    Elizabeth 3
    John 42
Brewster, Thomas 55
Brickell, Wright 25
Briscoe, Eliza Harris 62
    William 62
Broadwater, Guy 21
Broken, George 57
Brom, Thomas 33
Bronough, William 53
Brook, Deborah 13
Brooke, Elizabeth 13
    Hannah 13
Brooks, Aaron 51
    Hannah 5, 38, 51
    James 5
    Vincent, Ensign 56
    William 53
Broughton, Elizabeth 40
    William 27, 40
Brown, Aaron 44
    Abraham 48
    Andrew 18
    Ann 44
    Benjamin 25, 31, 49

    Betsy 11
    Catherine 32
    Coleman 34, 42
    Elizabeth 27, 44
    Fielding 59
    George 32, 44
    Hannah 32
    Henry 53, 55
    Hugh 53
    Isaac 31, 32, 35, 48
    Isacher 57
    Jacob 44
    James 10, 20, 50
    John 21, 32, 35, 44 (2), 48
    John A. 57
    John Alexander 13
    Joseph 5, 8, 42 ·
    Joseph Rhodes 29
    Leah 44
    Martha 35
    Mary 11, 29, 35
    Mercer 11
    Molly Middleton 5
    Moses 44
    Peter 24
    Rachel 44
    Richard 29, 42, 44
    Sarah 11, 44, 57
    Tamar 44
    Thomas 29, 32, 39, 42, 43, 44
    William 11, 12, 18, 20, 29 (2),
        32, 44, 47, 55
    Winnifred 49
Bryan, Thomas 55
Buchanan, William 51
Buckley, Elijah 36
    Elizabeth 10
    James 6
    John 10, 36
    Joshua 36, 47
    Reuben 10
    Samuel 36
    Scarlett 11
    William 36, 55
Buckner, Peyton 55
Bukley, Elizabeth 21
Burch, Edgar 62
    Mary Virginia 62
Burgoyne, Joseph 32
Burk, John 9
    Rhoda 9
Burks, Edward 21
Burnes, Joseph, Captain 56
Burns, J., Jr. 48
Burow, Joseph 16
Burson, Ann 6
    Benjamin 1, 6, 33, 39
    Catherine 39
    George 33, 39
    Hannah 39
    James 33, 48
    John 48
    Jonathan 33, 39, 48
    Joseph 6, 33
    Rebekka 32
    Sarah 33, 39
    Silas 39
Burton, Elizabeth 41
    William 53
Butcher, Elizabeth 14
    Jane 14
    John 14
    John, Sr. 14
    Samuel 14, 27
    Samuel, Jr. 14
    Susannah 14, 53
Butler, Jacob 57
    Lewis S. 53

Mary 57
Robert 57
Byland, David 13, 22
   Elizabeth 13
   Jesse 13
   Martha 13
   Rachel 13
   Samuel 13

--- C ---

Cadwallader, Jane 53
Caldwell, --- 59, 60
   Augusta 59
   Elizabeth 59
   Hugh 55
   Jean 42
   Joseph 2, 42
   Mary Elizabeth 59
   Moses 42
   S. B. T. 59
Callett, Alexander, 2nd Lt. 56
Camell, Jane 48
Campbell, Andrew 47
   Aneas 1
   Eneas (Enos) 55
   James 47 (2)
   Jane 48
   John 19, 44, 47, 52
   Marion 19
   Mathew 19
   Robert 25, 47
   Susannah 13
   William 47
Canby, Saml. 27
   Samuel 45
Canton, Elizabeth 31
   Mark 31
   Sarah 31
Capper, Frederick 30
Carlile, --- 53
   David 8, 36
   John 58
Carlyle, David 23
Carney, William 57
Carr, --- 59, 60
   Andrew 48
   Daniel 46
   Elizabeth 48
   James 48
   John 46, 48, 50, 53, 55
   Joseph 46, 48
   Margaret 48
   Mary 48
   Peter 46, 50
   Priscilla 59
   Sally 46
   Samuel 48
   Thomas 46, 48, 53
   Virginia Ellen 59
   William 46
Carrell, James 37
   William Porter 8
Carrill, David 58 (2)
Carrington, Timothy 38
   Winney K. 30
Carroll, Cynthia 13
   David 55
   Demse 13, 37
   Frances 13
   Mary Ann 13
   Rachel 13
   Rebecca 13
Carter, Edward 23, 24, 44
   Hannah 49
   James 49

John 37
Margaret 46
Peter 7, 53
William 45, 52
Castleberry, Sarah 9
Castleman, Massey 35
Catlett, Alexander, 2nd Lt. 56
Cavan, Neilson Patrick 19
   Patrick 23
Cavans, Patrick 18
Cavens, William, Ensign 56
   Williams, Captain 56
Cavin, Abraham 42
   John 25, 41
   Joseph 41
   Mary 41
   Patrick 23
   Robert 41
   William 17, 41, 42
Cavins, John 25, 43
   Joseph 53
   Patrick 18
   William 21
Chalfant, Robert 19
Chambers, Ann 1
   Veallator 1
   William 1, 55
Chamberlain, John 11
   Samuel 11
Chamblin, Ann 39
   Charles 39
   Jane Eleanor 39
   John 39
   Sarah 39
   William 39
Champe, Ann 3
   John 3
   Susy 3
   Thomas 3
Chancellor, Elizabeth Mildred 62
   Helen Ellzey 62
   Rush Wallace, Dr. 62
   Samuel 62
   Samuel Ashley 62
Chaney, Mary 7
Chapman, John 32
   Thomas 49
Cheve, Joseph 29
Chichester, Ann Thompson 62
   Arthur Mason, Capt. 62
   George Mason 62
Chick, William 49
Chilton, Ann 9, 10
   Elizabeth 3
   George 9, 21
   James 10
   John 9, 10, 35, 36, 40
   Mark 10
   Martha 10, 21
   Mary 9, 35
   Nancy 10
   Sarah 10, 35
   Steerman 35
   Sturman 3
   Thomas 9, 10, 35
   William 35
Chinn, Charles 7
   Christopher 7, 8, 21
   Elijah 7, 8, 22
   Elizabeth 7, 8
   John 7
   Raleigh 7
   Rawleigh 8
   Richard 53
   Thomas 7, 8, 21, 25
Christie, William, Capt. 28
Clack, Spebcer 8
Clagett, Charles 39

Mary Ann 39
Monica 39
Thomas 39
Claggett, --- 62, 64
   Haddie 62
   Lalla 61
   T. H. 64
   Thomas 62
   Thomas, Dr. 61 (2)
   Thomas H. 62
Clapham, J. 9
   Josias 9, 10, 20, 31, 34, 39 (2),
      51, 55
   P. 33
   Samuel 39
Clark, Ann 38
   Charles 8, 11
   Susanna 9
Clarke, Addison 59 (3)
   Eugenia 62
   Eve 39
   Isaac Vandevanter 59
   John 39
   Mary 59 (2)
Clary, Benjamin 55
Clauson, Cornelius 3
Claypole, James 29
   Joseph 29
Claypool, Joseph 55
Cleavland, William 35
Clendinen, Samuel 9
Clerk, Ann 38
Cleveland, Alexander 40
   Frances 40, 43
   George 40, 43
   Hannah 40
   James 40, 53
   James, Captain 56
   Johnson 43
   Johnston 40
Clevland, Darkes 35
   Mary 35
   William 35
Clewes, Thomas 55
Clews, Anna 41
   Elizabeth 41
   Joseph 29, 41
   Mary 41
   Nancy 41
   Phebe 41
   Ruth 41
   Thomas 29, 41
Climor, Christian 45
Cock, Catesby 58
Cocke, Catesby 58
   Lucy 45
   Washington 45
   William 31, 45
Cockerill, Benjamin 15
   Jeremiah 15
   John 15
   Sanford 15
   Thomas 15
Cockerille, Ann 35
   Anne 62
   Benjamin 30, 35
   Christopher 36, 48
   Jere 26
   Jeremiah 34, 42
   John 26, 35
   Lucy 62
   Richard 62
   William 41
Cockrell, Susannah 10
   Thomas 8
Colclough, widow 55
Cole, Mary 4, 11
   William 11

William 9
Delahand, John 60
Dement, Benoni 2
Dennington, George 6
Dent, Mary 8
    Rhoda 8
    William 8
Derry, Catherine 50
Dickey, James 15
Dillard, Ann 39
    James 11
    John 39
    William 11
Dillion, James 50
    John 31
Dillon, James 31, 34
    William 4, 6, 33
Dillons, James 43
Dixon, Hannah 35
    John 55
    Joist 55
Dodd, John 39
    William, Ensign 56
Donaldson, Ann 19
    Bayley 23
    Daniel 19
    Hugh 28
    James 4 (2)
    S.S. 15
    Sally 19
    Stephen 19
Donohoe, Margaret 40
Donohow, Margaret 1
Dormon, Hanson 55
Dorram, Mary Ann 60
    Thomas 60
Douglas, Ann 61
    Catherine 61
    Charles 61 (2)
    Elizabeth 28
    Hannah 28
    Hugh 28, 61 (2)
    Hugh, Captain 56
    Hugh, Ensign 56
    Hugh, 1st Lt. 56
    Louisa Ann 61
    Margaret 61
    Mary 49
    Nancy 28
    Patrick 28
    Peggy 28
    Sarah 28
    William 17, 18, 21, 23, 24, 25, 28
    William, Capt. 28
    William, Captain 56
Dowling, Daniel 40
Dowman, Raleigh 7
    William 7
Downs, James 59
Drake, --- 64
    Francis 62 (2), 64
    M.W. 64
    Mary Ann 62
Drane, Benjamin 15
    John 18
Drean, John 29
Dresh, Eleanor 59
Dudley, John 36
Dulin, Alfred 62 (3)
    Elizabeth 62
    Elizabeth Ann 62
    George Cephas 62
    Margaret 62
    Nancy 62
Duly, Charity 47
Dunbar, William, Jr. 32
Dunbarr, George 55

Duncan, Joshua 6, 22
Dunkin, Charles 46
Dunn, John 62
    Minnie 62
Durm, George 25
Durry, Catherine 50
Dutton, James 44
Dyal, William 10
Dyel, Elizabeth 4
    George 4
    James 4
    Josias 4
    Leonard 4
    Litter 4
    Rebecca 4
    Sarah 4
    Stacy 4
    Tibitha 4
    William 4
Dyer, Ann 4
    Hannah 32
    James 4
    John 32
Dykes, Anna 59

--- E ---

Eacha, Martana 28
Eaton, Mary 9
Eblens, Jane 42
Eblin, Elisha 39
    Hannah 39
    Isaac 39, 49
    Janet 39
    John 39, 49, 52
    Mary 39, 49
    Peter 39
    Samuel 39, 49
    Sarah 39
Echart, Adam 40
Eckhart, Adam 53
Ecton, Drucilla 30
    Theodore 30
Edelin, --- 53
Edwards, Amos 31
    Benjamin 2, 25, 44, 58
    Edward 46
Elgin, Charles 59
    Francis 20, 24, 55, 59
    Francis, Jr., Ensign 56
    George 20, 45
    Gustavus 20, 45
    Ignatus 20
    Jessy 20
    Margaret 20
    Nancy 20
    Rebecca 20
    Walter 20, 58
    William 20, 45
Ellgin, William 53
Elliott, Catherine 9
    James 45
    John 13, 25
    Thomasine 13
    Will 55
Ellis, Elias 5, 9, 13, 24, 26 (2)
    Ellis 50, 53
    Jesse 5
    Margaret 5
    Mary 5 (2)
    Nancy 5
    Rebecca 26
    Robert 5, 24
    Ruth 5
    Samuel 5
Ellzey, Lewis 47

    Lucy 47
    Margaret 47
    Sarah 47
    William 47
Elmere, John 57
Elmore, Genevie Mitchell 62
Elzey, John 30
    Lewis 30
    Lydia 30
    Prudence 30
    Thomas 17
Emery, George 23, 29
    Stephen 25, 28
English, Susannah 34
Eskridge, Ann 16
    Charles 26, 34, 44, 55
    Charles, Col. 34
    Charles, Major 16, 56
    William 46
Ethel, John 4
    Winnifred 4
Ethell, John 5
    Winnifred 5
Evan, Will 55
Evans, Alexander 17
    Catherine 8
    David 5, 11
    Elizabeth 5, 10, 17, 22
    George 48
    Griffin 3
    Griffith 5
    John 5, 8 (2), 11
    Jonathan 8
    Joshua 5, 10, 11, 25
    Martha 11
    Mary 5, 8 (3), 10, 30, 36 (2), 55
    Oliver 8
    Price 8
    Richard 5
    Samuel 8, 36
    Sarah 8, 48
    William 5, 8, 10, 11, 12, 36, 53
    Zachariah 17
Evens, Peggy 46
Everhard, Charlotta 9
    Elizabeth 9
    Jacob 9
Everts, Charles 62
    Mollie 62
Evins, John 20, 22
    Mary 20

--- F ---

Fairfax, --- 62 (2)
    Elizabeth 62
    Eugenia 62 (3)
    Henry 62 (5)
    John Walter 62
    Lindsay 62
    William 20
Fairhurst, Jeremiah 55
    John 41
Fan, Jacob 55
Fanihevist, George 39
Farnsworth, John 57
Farpain, Mary 53
Farrow, Elizabeth 29
    Joseph 25, 29, 51, 53
    Mary Ann 29
    Sarah 29
    Thomas 29
    Thornton 29
    William 29
Fauch, Ann 6
    Jacob 6

Susannah 6
Faunce, Nicholas 24
Fauntleroy, Charles M., Col.
    59 (2)
    Janet 59
    T.T., Gen. 59
Feagan, Daniel 31
Fearst, Christian 52, 53
    Hannah 52
Feebe, John 10
Feirst, Christian 12
    John 12
    Peter 12
Fenly, Patrick 33
Field, Jamima 42
    Jemima 18, 43
    John 4, 18
    Thomas 18
    William 18, 50
Fielder, Hizziah 37
Fields, Elizabeth 28
    John 5, 16
    Thomas 16, 23
    William 16
Fierst, Ann 11
    Christian 11
    Elizabeth 11
    John 11
    Peter 11, 25
    Sarah 11
Filler, Andrew 28
Filles, Andrew 28
Fine, Catherine 52
    Peter 52, 53
Fishburne, --- 62
Fitchelharles, Phillipina 50
Fitchet, Naomi 59
Fitzgerald, John, Col. 16
Fitzsimmons, Mary 45
Fletcher, Nancy 33
    Sarah Newell 33
    William 33
Floyd, Sarah 30
    William 38
Foreman, Peter 30
Forg, Frances 7
Forres, Murray 61
Foster, Jesse 2
Fouch, Abraham 18
    Ann 51
    Daniel 45
    George 45
    Hugh 18
    Isaac 45, 55
    Isaac, Jr. 37, 40
    Jacob 18
    Jonathan 18, 40, 45
    Mary 18, 45
    Thomas 37, 40, 45
    William 45
    Zach 18
Fouche, H. 28
Foutch, Mary 1
Foutt, George 29
Foutts, Elizabeth 29
    Eve 29
    Frederick 29
    George 29
    Hannah 29
    Philip 29
Fowkes, Robert 51
    Robert D. 53
Fox, Absalom 16
    Amos 26, 35, 43
    Ann 13
    Anna 16
    Bartleson 45
    Catherine 49

Elizabeth 12
Gabriel 13, 16, 18
George 35
George W. 58
James 12, 20
Mary 49
William 9, 10, 12, 13, 16, 18,
    23, 43, 45, 49 (2)
Frahern, James 19
    Rebecca 19
    Sarah 19
    William 19
Francis, Thomas 58
Frazier, James 18
Frean, Peter 41
Fred, Frank 62
Frederick, Annie P. 62
    Frank L. 62
Freeman, Anna 62
    Hezekiah 39
    Mary 39
Frier, Daniel 9
    Hannah 9
    James 8, 9 (2)
    Pheby 9
    Robert 9, 19
Fry, Henry 26
    Nicholas 57
Frye, Frederick 62
Fryer, James 23
    Robert 11
Fulkner, Benjamin 53
Fulton, David 51
    James 51
    John 51
    Lenah 51
    Milly 51
    Robert 14, 51, 53
    Robt. 53
    Sarah 48
Funkhouser, --- 62
    Frank 62 (2)
    Mary Benjamin 62
Furr, Enoch, 1st Lt. 56

--- G ---

Gallenher, David 46
    William 46
Gardner, Catherine 59
    E. 35
    Elender 3
    Joseph 31, 51
    Mary 10, 11
    Mary E. 59
Garner, Catherine 59
    James 59 (2)
    Margaret 59
    Silvester 55
Garrett, Edward 55
Garrison, N. 29
    Nehemiah 29
Gault, William 53
Geesling, Ann 16
George, Jonathan 41
    Thomas 5, 6, 21, 53
    William 49
    William, Captain 56
Gess, John 3
Ghorman, Margaret 35
Gibbs, Ann 11
    James 27
    William 11
Gibson, Aaron 38
    Dinah 38
    Ealse 38

Isaac 38
James 38
Jesse 38
John 38
Jonathan 38
Joseph 38
Miriam 38
Moses 38
Rachel 38
Ruth 38
Susan 38, 62
Susannah 64
Thomas 15, 38
William 38
Gidding, A.E. 62
    James 62
    Susan 62
    William 62 (3)
Gideon, Peter 58
Gilbert, Joseph 29
    Silas, Ensign 56
Gilmore, Elizabeth 57, 60
    William 57
Gist, Constant 15
    Elizabeth 46
    Henson 15
    Henson Lewis 15
    John 15, 24
    Mary 15
    Nathaniel 15
    Sarah 15
    Thomas 15
    William 15
Goard, Joshua 55
Goff, Adam 57
Gold, Ann 47
    Joseph 47
Goley, Thomas 51
Goodens, Amos 53
Goodin, Amos 7
    David 7 (2), 31
    John 7
    Kesiah 7
    Martha 7
    Rebecca 7
    Samuel 7, 31
    Sarah 7
Gooding, Anna 34
Gooley, Thomas 53
Gordon, Mary 38 (2)
    Robert 23
Gore, Ann 33
    Anne 38
    Betsy 31
    Elizabeth 38
    Hannah 38
    John 42
    Jonathan 31
    Joseph 39, 41, 42 (2)
    Joshua 18, 31, 37, 38, 55
    Mark 38
    Rowena 59
    Sarah 37
    Thomas 31, 33, 38, 40, 55, 58
Gorham, Ann 10
    Harving 10
    Lamken 10
    Sanford 10
    Thomas 12, 25
    William 10
Gorr, Joshua 31
Gose, Joshua 29
    Sarah 29
Gossitt, William 2
Gotcley, Elizabeth 3
Grady, James 14, 50
Graham, John 20, 36
Graves, William 7

Gray, H.B. 61
   Haddie 62
   Henrietta 61
   Isabella 61
   John 61 (3)
   Rebecca 61
Grayson, Benjamin 1
   Spencer 17
Grecelius, Rudolph 9
Green, Ann 48
   Fielding 48
   Frances 48, 49
   George 49
   Gerrard 49
   Richard 22, 24
   Ruth 2
   Thomas 48, 49, 58
   William 48
Greenup, Christopher 27, 29
Greenwood, Caleb 8
Gregg, --- 41
   Amos 35
   Amy 35
   Dinah 41
   George 2, 8, 35, 55 (2)
   Isaac 41
   John 32, 35, 41, 43, 46, 55
   Joseph 33, 41
   Levi 43
   Levy 35, 41
   Mary 35, 41 (2)
   Michael 55
   Nathan 47
   Rebecca 33, 35
   Richard 35
   Samuel 22, 35, 41, 47, 55
   Stephen 32, 47
   Susan 47
   Susannah 47
   Thomas 41, 47, 53, 55
   William 41, 50
Griffith, Charles G. 4
   Daniel 12
   Evan 53
   George 55
   John 29
   Mary 9
   Rebecca 29
   Richard 52
   Sarah 9
   Thomas 58
   William 25
Grigg, George 6
   Martha 31
Griggs, Elias 43
   Elizabeth 43 (2)
   George 43
   Hannah 43
   Mary 43
   Ruth 43
   Samuel 11
   Sarah 43
   William 43
Grigsby, James 50 (2), 53
   Nathaniel 1
Grimes, Edward 4
   Nicholas 4
   Nicholas, Sr. 4
   Philip 4
   William 4, 51
Grove, Elizabeth 3
   William 3
Groves, William 7
Grymes, Anna 51
   Edward 51
   Jain 51
   John 51
   Nicholas 51

Sanford 51
Silvester 51
Gun, John 53
Gunnell, Elizabeth 20
   Henry 48
   Henry, Jr. 48
   John 17, 48
   William 25, 30
Guthry, Thomas 1

--- H ---

Hackney, Sarah 1
Haddocks, John 15
Haden, Barbesheba 32
   John 32
Hagarman, Adrian 52
Hague, Ann 5, 18
   Frances 43
   Francis 2, 5 (2), 13, 18, 26, 35,
      55 (2)
   Hannah 18
   Isaac 5, 11, 18, 35, 43
   John 5, 30, 55
   Jonah 5
   Joseph 5
   Mary 18
   Rebecca 18
   Samuel 5, 18
   Sarah 18, 45
   Thomas 18, 43
Haiden, Charles 43
Haines, Simeon 29
Hains, --- 41
   Hephyidah 52
   Mary 52
   Sarah 52
   Simeon 52
   Stacy 52
   Thomas 52, 53
   William 52
Halbert, Ailsy 47
   James 47
   Katy 47
   Lydia 47
   Michael 47, 53
   Rosannah 36
   Rosey 47
   Sally 47
   Thomas 47
   William 47
Hale, Levi 48
Hall, Amy 17
   Betsy 7
   Eliza Ann 59
   James 4
   John 7
   Jonathan 40
   Mary 17, 48, 59
   Richard 44
   West John 3
   William 59
   William, Jr. 55
Halling, Jemima 33
   John 33
   John Wilcoxen 33, 43
   William 33
Hambey, John 55
   Will 55
Hambrey, --- 55
Hamby, John 4, 55
Hamilton, David 57
   Elizabeth 12
   James 3, 12, 23, 53, 55, 58
   Jane 14, 57
   John 12, 42

   Mary 12
   Robert 7, 14, 25
Hammet, George 35
Hammitt, Sarah 51
Hammond, Ellen Roberta 62
Hampton, Elizabeth 3
   Mary 46
Hamrick, J. 5
   James 5
Hamten, Elizabeth 41
Hanbey, James D. 63
Hancock, Althea 10
   Simon, Captain 56
   William 2
Hancocke, Mary 18
   William 18
Hand, Petee 53
Handley, John J. 63
   Sarah 63
Hanks, Elizabeth 10
Hanly, John 53
Hanson, Gustavous 44, 53
   Sarah 44
Hanvey, James D. 63
Harbert, Peter 44
Harden, Elihu 43
   Thomas 9
Harding, Elihu 48
Hardy, Joshua 46
Harle, Elizabeth 48
   John 48, 55
Harley, Elizabeth 48
Harman, Peter 41
Harper, Mary Amelia 63
   Robert 63 (2)
   William 11
Harris, --- 64
   Ann 3, 12
   Catherine 36
   David 3
   Eliza 62, 63
   Elizabeth 12, 36
   Henry 57
   Jacob 12
   John 12, 18, 26
   Joseph 3
   Mary 8, 28
   Richard Lee 63
   Samuel 3, 8, 28, 55
   Sarah 19, 36, 63
   Sophia 57
   Thomas 28
   William 3, 21, 28, 55, 62
   William B. 63
   William Briscoe 63
Harrison, A... Blackburn 61
   Anne Maria 61
   Burr 8
   Burr W. 61
   Edward Burr 61
   Elizabeth Conrad 61
   John 18
   Peyton 8
   Sally 61 (2)
   Sarah P. 61
   W.B. 61
   W. Burr 61
   William Burr 61 (2)
Harrys, David 55
Harst, John 12
Hartman, Catherine 28
   Mathais 28
Hartsel, Robert 63
Harvin, Edward 58
Hatcher, James 21, 55
   John 35, 55
   Joshua 44
   William 58

Hatchner, William 55
Hatfield, Thomas 4
Hatton, Thomas 33
Havener, Virginia 63
   W. D. 63 (2)
Hawkins, John 46
Hawley, John 44, 48
Hawling, Elizabeth 59
   Hannah 59 (2)
   J. Lewis 63 (2)
   John 3, 59 (3)
   John Wilcoxen 4
   Martha 63
   Mary 59
Haynie, Bridger 3
Hays, Nancy 37
   William 37
Head, Benjamin 39
   George 60
   John 53
   Mary 60
Headen, George 48
   Philip 3
   Samuel 34
Headon, Jennie 34
Heale, Kitty 28
Heaslip, Isabelle 61
Heater, Richard 63
Heath, Andrew 48
Hedges, Richard 27
Helm, Joseph, Rev. 63 (2)
   Louis 63
   Mary 63
   Mary Clarke 63
   Meredith 36
Helms, Mary 42
   Meredith 42
Henderson, Adam 57
   Catherine 57
   Edward 61
   Hugh 57
   Ora 61
   Samuel 36
Hendrick, Roberta Leckie 63
Henning, Mary 14
Henry, John 32
   Joseph 53
Herbert, Josias 42
Hereford, John 27
Hereman, Helen 30
   William 30
Heryford, John 22, 55
Hetherby, Thomas 18
Hewelson, Benjamin 18
Hews, Edward 5
Hewston, Benjamin 32
Hickman, Conrad 52
Hickmon, Conrad 53
Hide, Philip 39
Higgins, Dennie 63
   Mary Catherine 63
Hiler, Michael 17
Hill, Margaret 57
   Richard 57
Hillard, Ann Eliza 60
   Joseph 60 (2)
   Sophia 60
Hillfine, Nancy 46
Hilliard, John 57
Hilt, Samuel 25
Hinds, John 53
Hirsh, John 13
Hirst, John 36
   Mary 36
Hitch, Thomas 19
Hixen, Timothy 13
   William 13
Hixon, James 58

   William 18, 50, 53
Hixson, Timothy, Captain 56
Hogan, James 63
   Thomas 3
Hoge, James 37 (2)
   Morgan 37
   Rebekah 37
   Sol. 21
   Solomon 37
Hogeland, James 58
Hogen, Thomas 13
Hoges, George 37
   James 37
   Solomon 37
   William 37
   Zebulon 37
Hogue, Francis 2
   Isaac 38
   John 36
   Solomon, Jr. 31
Hole, Mary 42
Holland, Eliner 37
Hollingsworth, Ann 1
   Jonah 1
   Lydia 1
   Phebe 1
   Rachel 1
Hollins, William 55 (2)
Holme, William 3
Holmes, Deborah 12
   Joshua 12
   Margaret 12
   Mary 12
   Rachel 12
   Sarah 12
   William 12, 22, 37
Holton, Thomas 33
Homan, Ann 9
   Elizabeth 51
   Hannah 51
   Mark 51
   Mary 51
   Mathew 51
   Reuben Stephens 51
Homasn, Ralph 35
Hooe, John 30
Hook, Isaac 34
   Mary 34
Hooten, Sarah 31
Hopewell, Ann 16
   Hannah 4
   John 4
   Thomas 4
Hophpoch, Alie Mary 17
   Cornelius 17
Hopkin, James 18
Hopkins, Benj. 53
   David, Ensign 56
   John 55
Hopoch, Cornelius 24
Hoppoch, Alice 53
   Mary 41
Hough, Amos 49
   Ann 14
   Benjamin 49 (2)
   Bernard 58
   Brand 14
   Coleman 14
   Daniel 32
   Hugh 14
   James 14
   John 1 (2), 5, 14, 18, 49, 53,
     55, 58
   Jonah 49
   Joseph 14, 23
   Joseph, Ensign 56
   Mahlon 49
   Mary 49

   Rachel 49
   Samuel 29, 49
   Sarah 14, 49
   William 49
   William, Jr. 14
   William, Sr. 14
Houghman, Charity 17
Houghton, Elijah 46
Householder, Adam 32
Howard, John 59
Howell, Abner 8, 13
   Andrew 13
   Ann 13, 43
   Benjamin 13
   Daniel 13
   Deborah 43
   Hugh 13
   John 13, 57
   Lydia 35
   Mahlon 43
   Margaret 13
   Martha 35
   Phebe 43
   Rachel 13
   Reuben 13
   Samuel 43, 53
   Thomas 43
   Timothy 12, 43, 50, 53
   William 13, 35
Howling, John Wilcoxen 4
Howman, Elizabeth 17
Huey, Mary 42
Huffman, Anthony 17, 49
   Henry 41
   John 41
   Margaret 41
   Peter 41
   Philip 41
Huffty, Benjamin 50
Hugeley, Abraham 40
   Charles 41, 52, 53
   Charles, Sr. 50
   George 41, 50
   Jacob 41
   Job 50
   John 50
   Mary 50
   Polly 41
Hughes, Constantine 44
   Elizabeth 11, 39
   Isaac 28
   Margaret 11
   Mary 11
   Rachel 11
Hulls, Elizabeth 3
Humphrey, Isaac 53
   Jane 59
   John 33
   Thomas 26, 33, 37
   Thomas, Jr. 37
   William 37
Humphreys, Abner 47
   Mary 35
   Thomas 35, 47 (2)
Humphries, Susannah 40, 43
Hunt, Christopher 20
   Lewis 59
   Stephen 20
   William 53
Hunter, Sarah Wallace 64
Huppoch, Cornelius 49
   Elsey 49
   John 49
   Peter 49
Hurst, Jemimah 3
Hutcheson, William 36
Hutchins, Joshua 49
Hutchinson, Benjamin 48, 55

Daniel 55
Isaac 34 (2)
James 46
Jere 55
Jeremiah 46
John 55
Joseph 55
Hutchison, Andrew 58
Benj. 53
Benjamin 23, 53
Daniel 58
Elizabeth 35
George 35
Jere. 44
Jereimah 7
Jeremiah 3, 15, 43
Jeremiah, Sr. 49
John 7, 44, 58
Joseph 35
Sarah 49
William, Ensign 56
Hutton, John 10
Joseph 10
Saml. 53
Sarah 10
Thomas 10
Hychew, Jacob 13
Nicholas 13

--- I ---

Iden, John 58
Sam 53
Inslee, Henry 2
Mary 2
William 2
Inzer, George 63
Irvin, Samuel 32

--- J ---

Jack, John 29
Nancy 29
Patrick 31
Patrick, M.D. 29
Jackson, Abigail 46
Alexis 1
Ann 46
Benjamin 63
Charles F. 63
Daniel 31
Elizabeth Clapham 63
Febe 46
George 63
Henry 1, 63
James 46
John 46
John, Jr. 15
Lovell 5, 55
Martha 42
Rebecca 63
Rebecca T. 63
Richard 46
Samuel Clapham 63
Sarah 46
Thomas 12
William 46 (2), 63 (3)
Jacobs, Ann 6
Jacob 18
Jacoby, Ann 50
Jacob 50
James, Anne 37
Charles E. 63 (2)
Dora Esther 63

Elias 37
Ernest 63
Hannah 37
Isaac 37
Jacob 46
James 37
Margaret 47
Sarah 63
Stephen 11
Thomas 37
Jameson, Robert 26
Jamison, Robert 12, 16
Janney, --- 58
Abel 1, 13, 19, 22, 31, 38,
    39 (2), 43
Abel, Jr. 12
Abel, Sr. 55
Abell 58
Alice 63
Amos 13
Ann 55
Aquilla 33
Blackstone 33, 39
Charles Philip 63
Cornelia 13
Elisha 33, 39
Eliz. 53
Elizabeth 39, 42, 50
Hannah 33, 42
Isaac 39
Israel 19, 33, 43, 47
Jacob 12, 19, 29, 33, 55, 58
Jacob B. 55
Jane 18
Jesse 39, 47
John 31, 42, 53, 63 (2)
Jonas 33
Joseph 1, 11, 12, 13, 14, 19, 31,
    33, 42, 55, 58
Macey 39
Mahlan 19
Mahlon 5, 13, 19, 33, 38, 42,
    45, 50, 55, 58 (2)
Mary 5, 13, 42
Mel 12
Mocahlon 13
Moses 33
Rebecca 31, 42
Ruth 5, 13
Samuel 5, 19, 31
Sarah 31, 42
Stacey 39
Susannah 42
Thomas 33, 42
William 39
Janny, Blackstone 12
Jared, John 12
Jenkin, David 6, 14
Margaret 14
Mary 14
Jenkins, Alice 51
Amos 26
Charles 48
Daniel 11
David 26
Isaac 14, 32
John 14, 22, 30, 48, 50, 53
John, Sr. 11
Lena 30
Nancy 37
Philip 34
Priscilla 33
Samuel 1
Stephen 33
Sylvanus 30
Sylvester 48
William 26, 48
Jenney, Mary 1

Rebecca 1
Jenning, James 7
Jennings, Ann 28
Anna 49
Daniel 23, 28
James 17 (2), 28
Jeremiah 28
Owen 28
William 28
Jett, Anna Raney 15
Jewell, Jonathan 36
John, Daniel 6
Dinah 6
Hannah 6
James 5
John 6
Martha 6
Mary 5 (2), 6
Sarah 6
Thomas 6, 8, 55, 58
Johnson, --- 20
Bayley 7
James 20
Jeffrey 3
John 7, 20, 24
Mary 7, 53
Smith 7
Johnston, --- 20
Archibald 14
Betty 14
Dennis McCarty 14
George 14
George, Col. 24
George, Dr. 45
Wilford 14
William 48
Jones, Amos 53
Ann 13, 53
Catherine 63
Elizabeth 3
James 9
John 27 (2), 28 (2), 63
Joseph 28
Joshua 9
Martha 28
Richard 63
William 2, 5, 8, 9, 28
Jordan, Ann 3
George 3
Jordon, Angels 53
Angus 53

--- K ---

Kailer, Barbara 43
Hannah 43
Keen, Ann 16
Elender 15
Elizabeth 15
Francis 16, 23
James 16
John 16, 23, 55
Mary 15, 16
Richard 16
Sarah 16
Kelley, Charles 63
Hattie E. 63
James 53
Thomas 1
Kelly, John 39
Kent, John 47
Susannah 47
Kenworthy, William 33, 37
Kephart, --- 63 (2)
Barbara 63 (2)
Eugenia 63

George 63
Margaret 63
Marion 63
Kernans, Thomas, 2nd Lt. 56
Kevens, John 6
Kilgore, George 9, 15, 24, 43
George, 1st Lt. 56
Kimblar, John 41
Kimblars, John 41
Sarah 41
King, Benjamin 47 (2)
Daniel 47
Elizabeth 38
Hannah 4
Herman, 2nd Lt. 56
John 4, 29, 30, 38, 47
John, Jr. 32
Mary 30, 38
Micajah Watkins 63
Osborn 4, 38
Osborne 30
Richard 57
Sarah 30, 38, 51
Smith 19, 25, 30, 31, 38
Smith, 2nd Lt. 56
Thomas, Capt. 56
Thomas, 1st Lt. 56
William 47, 55
Winny 38
Kiphard, Godfrey 44
Kirk, James 18, 19 (2), 23
William 11, 55
Kirkbridge, Mahlon 55
Kirkpatrick, John Thomas 63
Marvin 63
Mary Della 63
Kitchen, Daniel 36
James 31
Margaret 36
Thompson 36
William 36, 37
Kitchens, William 22
Kitzmiller, Elizabeth 59
Martin 59 (2)
Kiwan, William 44
Kline, John N. 58
Knox, Catherine 59
Thomas 59 (2)

--- L ---

Lacey, Charles H. 59
Lacy, James 53
Joseph 54
Laid, John 15
Lains, Thomas 46
Lake, Elizabeth 8
Mary 17
Lamb, Thomas 2
Lamy, Peter 43
Lance, Peter 20
Land, Ann 8
Carr Wilson 8
Isaac 9
James 8
Joseph 8
Pressley Carr 8
Sally 8
William Carr 8
Landin, Barthany 14
Lane, Aaron 9, 40
Andrew 54
C. Wilson 54
Daniel C. 34
Delilah 34
Elizabeth 34

Enoch Smith 34
George 34
Hardage 7, 30, 40
James 5 (2), 15, 26, 43, 52, 54,
55
James, Esq., Major 26
James, Maj. 44
James H. 34
James Hardage 34 (2)
John 34
Lydia 40
Mary 34 (2)
Rebecca 34
Sally 16
Sarah 40
Will 26
William 14, 15, 25, 34, 36, 40,
47
William, Jr. 44
William, Sr., Captain 56
William Carr 8, 36
William Carr, Capt. 7
Lanes, John 11
Langley, John 1
Lanham, Aaron 46
Aquilla 46
Eleanor 46
Elizabeth 46
Hezekiah 46
Ladock 46
Lethe 46
Mercy Ann 46
Walter 46
Lapon, Thomas 10
Lassure, Andrew 57
Laswell, Jacob 55
Lawerence, Moses 33
Lawrason, James 19
Lay, Abraham 30, 54
Emmanuel 30
Joseph 30
Marmaduke 30
Sarah 30
Silvester 4
Stephen 30, 51
Sylvania 30
Sylvester 22
Laycock, Adin 63 (2)
John B. 63
John William 63
Lawerence 63
Margaret M. 63
Margaret Morton 63
Mary 63
Lease, Catherine 43
George 43
John 43
Leckie, Roberta 63
Lee, A. D., Rev. 63
Elizabeth 63
George, Dr. 61
Henry, Col. 30
Ludwell 58
Maria 61
Nannie 63
Leech, George 3
Leis, George 24
Leitch, James 54
Jesse 54
Lemert, Lewis 19
Lese, Bartholomew 17
Catrean 17
Dorety 17
Dorothy 17
George 17
Hannah 17
John 17
Joseph 17

Lester, Hugh 51
Letch, Isaac 12
Jesse 12
Letcher, --- 61
Ann Eliza Moffett 63
Charles 63 (2)
Levering, Alice 19
Griffith 19
Mary 19
Septimus 19
Thomas 19
Lewellin, Mary 32
Thomas 6
Lewelyn, Thomas 14
Lewis, Abraham 54
Ann 49
Betty 42
Charles 44 (2), 48, 49, 50, 51
Daniel 51
Daniel, 2nd Lt. 56
George 6, 15, 24, 27, 31, 49, 50
George A. 47
James 32, 49, 50, 52, 54
Joel 31, 33
John 2, 6, 9, 13, 21, 25, 42, 49
John, Sr. 55
Joseph 15, 24, 27, 49, 52
Levi 13
Mary 5, 46
Nathan 15, 24
Rebecca 42
Sarah 13, 53
Stephen 15
Thomas 4, 5, 9, 22, 26, 37, 55
Thomas, Captain 56
Thomas, Jr. 22
Thomas, Sr. 22
Vilet 15
Vincent 2, 25, 27, 49, 54, 55
William 9
Lickey, George 59
Mary 59
Lies, George 24
Lightfoot, ---, widow 29
Benjamin 29
Liken, James 14
William 14
Lindsay, Abraham 55
Martha 20
Thomas 20
Linn, Mathew 1
William 12
Linton, Ann 10, 46
Caty 46
Edward 1
John 7, 20, 24 (2), 27, 28, 51
John, Captain 56
Littlejohn, John 18, 40, 44, 51
Monica 18
Littler, William 41
Littleton, Charles 14
Edgar 63
Elizabeth 63 (3)
Elizabeth Buffington 63
Emma 63
F. B. 63
John 14
John, Ensign 56
Mary 42
Solomon 51
Thomas 63 (5)
Virginia 63
William 2 (2), 14, 21, 43
Locker, John 47
Lodge, Icabod 14
Isabell 26
William 14
Loftin, Daniel 27

Lofton, Daniel 27
Long, Ada White 64
    Isaac 64
    Jacob 58
    James 4
    Thomas 4
Lott, Mary Smalle 64
    Parkinson 64
Lovatt, Daniel 31
    David 31
    Edmund 31
    Elias 31
    Elizabeth 31
    Jonathan 31
    Joseph 31
    Letisha 31
    Lidia 31
    Sarah 31
Love, Samuel 31
    Samuel, Jr. 34
Lovell, Jonathan 49
Lovett, Jonathan 33, 41, 44
    Nancy 41
    William 57
Low, Elizabeth 15
Lowden, Mary 64
Lowell, Thomas 22
Lucas, Alexander 14, 25
    Cassandra 14
    Ruth 18
    Samuel 27
Luckett, Charity 3
    Elizabeth 45
    John 34, 39, 45
    Lawson 34
    Molly Ann 31, 45
    Otho 34
    Philip 45
    Thomas 34
    Thomas Huzza 34
    Val 34
    William 3
    William, Jr. 3, 4
    William, Sr. 4
Luke, Elizabeth 45
Lutesinger, Michael 13
    Philip 13
    Rebecca 13
    Sarah 13
Lloyd, David 29
Lyles, Eleanor 10
Lynham, Philip 2
Lynn, Mary 10

--- M ---

Mackall, Benjamin 39
Madden, Sarah 52
Magill, Anne 59
Mahue, James 43
    Moses 43
Mains, --- 60 (2)
    Mary 59
    Washington 59
    William 48, 59 (2)
Major, Daniel 49
    Elijah 49
    Elizabeth 49
    Hannah 64
    James 49
    Richard 49
    Richard, Rev. 40
    Sarah 49
Mangold, Valentine 12
Marcy, Charles 1
Mark, Elisha 7, 33

Marks, Abel 33, 35
    Elisha 33, 35
    Elisha, Captain 56
    Elisha, Ensign 56
    Isaiah 33
    John 33, 35
    John, Sr. 35
    Miriah 35
    Thomas 33, 35, 38
    Ureah 35
Marlow, Anna Fox 64
    Edward 64 (2)
Marshall, F. 54
    James 9, 15, 16, 42, 51
    Joseph 5, 42
    Rachel 16
    Samuel 16, 42 (2)
    Thomas 54
    William 42
Marten, James 18
Martial, James 9
    Joseph 9
    Margaret 9
    Martha 9
    Mary 9
    Rachel 9
    Robert 9
    Samuel 9
    Susannah 9
Martin, Elizabeth 48
    James 14
    John 9, 25
    Joseph 9
    Mary 9, 52
    Ralph 9, 21
    Sarah 48
    Thomas 9, 48
    Uphemia (Euphemia) 14
    William 9, 14
Mason, Abraham 49
    Ann 46
    Benjamin 2, 20, 24, 25,
       27 (3), 40, 43, 46
    Burgess 46
    George 20, 46
    John 46
    Margaret 20, 46
    Mary 46
    Sally Inness 61
    Sarah 49
    Steven 61
    Thompson 62
    Thomson 13
    William 46
    William, 1st Lt. 56
    William T. 61
    William T., Ensign 56
    William W. 46
    Woolverton 46
Massey, Lee 2, 8, 55
Masterson, Mary 3
    Sarah 11
Mathew, Thomas 12
Matile, E. Albert 64
    Flora 64
    James 64
Matthew, Simon 54
Matthews, Peter 39
    Susannah 8
Matton, Ambrose 52
    Ann 52
    Israel 52
    Mary 52
    Sarah 52
Mayor, Richard 54
McCabe, Henry 18, 19, 27, 44, 51,
    54
    William 42, 44

McCaney, Mary 10
McCarty, John 1
McClain, Duncan 35
McClelan, Sarah 12
    William 12, 22
McCleland, Robert 12
    William 12
McConley, Elizabeth 42
McConochee, James 25
McCoy, William 1
McCullah, Robert 44
McDonough, James 59
McDowell, Ann 1
    James 55
    Jean 1
McElroy, Daniel 35
    Rebekka 35
McGeach, Ann 6
    Elizabeth 6
    James 6
    Jane 6
    John 6
    Joseph 2, 6, 55
    Thomas 6
    William 6
McGeath, James 40
    William 50, 54
McGinnis, Edward 50
    Jean 50
McGrew, Charles 4
    James 4
    John 4
McGrews, Charles 4
    Elizabeth 4
    James 4
    John 4
    Robert 4
McIlhaney, Hannah 10
    James 10
    John 10
    Mary 10
    Rachel 10
    Rosanna 10
    Thomas 10
McIllaheny, John 2
McIllhaney, James 16, 30
    James, Captain 56 (2)
    James, Major 56
McIllhany, Elizabeth 61
    James 61 (2)
    Margaret 61
McInhaney, James 10
McIntosh, Thomas 30
McItheney, John 2
McKim, Alexander 41
    James 41
McKinley, Mary 50
    William 50
McKinney, George 9
McKnight, William 26, 43
McLaughlin, Amos (Amon) 31
McLean, Duncan 38
    John, Ensign 56
    Mary 38
McMakin, Alexander 24
McNealey, Mary 64
McPherson, Ann 52
    Daniel 52
    Jesse 52
    John 52
    Joseph 52
    Lucy 64
    Mathew 64 (2)
    Stephen 52
    Stephens 54
    William 52
McVey, Patrick 17
Mead, Ann 29, 35

Anne 35
Benjamin 44
Christiana 29
Ellen 35
John 55
Mary 40
Samuel 12, 58
William 2, 29 (2), 36, 55, 58
William, Jr. 5
William, Sr. 5
Megeagh, Mary 2
Megeah, Anne 2
Elizabeth 2
Jane 2
Jonathan 2
Joseph 2
Thomas 2
Mellan, Thomas, Ensign 56
Mercer, E.W. 64
George Stuart 64
Lee Washington 64
Martha E. 64
Meredith, Elizabeth 43
Mershon, Joseph 49
Thomas 49
Metcalf, John 7
Meville, Ruth 52
Meyers, George 42
Mary Barbara 42
Meyrick, Griffith 8
James 8
John 8
Susannah 8
Middleton, Hannah 5
Jane 5
John 55
Lettice 5
Mary 48
William 49
Milholland, Patrick 54
Millan, Hannah 16
Thomas 32
Millane, Thomas 32
Miller, Bazella 46
C. 54
Catherine 6
Christian 12
Daniel 31
Jane 10
John 5 (2), 6
Sinthy 46
Millian, William 26
Milner, Percy 64
Gertrude Ball 64
Miner, Elizabeth 42
Mary 10
Nicholas 42
Minn, Michael 2
Minor, America Spencer 64
Elizabeth 42
Frances 18, 20 (2)
George 20
James 64
John 18 (2), 19, 20
Joseph 54
Michael, Jr., Ensign 56
Nicholas 19, 20, 58 (7)
Nicholas, Col. 55
Rebecca 20
Spencer 20 (2), 28, 44, 54
Stewart 20
Thomas 19, 20, 28
Thomas, Ensign 56
Mitchell, Adam 21
Mitinger, Daniel 17
Mittinger, Daniel 16
Mobley, Mary 6
Samuel 6

Moffett, Ann Eliza 63
Benjamin 40
Beulah 64
Elizabeth 40
Henry 54
Joseph 31
Nancy 40
Paul 64
Robert 40
Thomas 64 (2)
Vylinda H. Rush 64
William 20
Molton, Mary 27
Money, Mary 15
Nicholas 15, 30
Rachel 15
Monhane, Joseph 28
Monies, John 34
Nancy 34
Monkhouse, Jonathan 27
Monroe, Sarah 6
Monrow, Fillis 6
George 6
Rosannah 6
Sarah 6
Moore, A. 42
Ann 19 (2), 37
Ann Mason 61
Asa 52
Benjamin 36, 38
Cloe 46
Elizabeth Mary 19
Francis 48
Hannah 62
Henry 55
Jacob 38
James 37, 42, 50, 52
Jeremiah 19, 35
John 36, 38, 50
Thomas 17, 54
Thomas, Jr. 37
Thomas Neale 19
Thompson W. 61
Westwood Thompson 61
William 6, 38
Moralee, Sophia 60
Sarah 60
Thomas 60
Morehane, Joseph 18
Morgerts, Philip 25
Morgin, Philip 20
Morin, Daniel 7
James 7
John 7
Joseph 7
Katy 7
Molly 7
Nancy 7
Peggy 7
Prudence 7
Morris, Benjamin 3
Jacob 23
Rebecca 3
Samuel 3
Morse, John 58
Mortimer, Bethelmere 17
Infamous 17
Sarah 17
William 16
Morton, Edward 55
Thomas 55
Mosgrove, William 2
Mosley, Samuel 52
Moss, Elizabeth 5
Frances 5, 11
Gideon 30
Hannah 5
John 5, 8, 9 (2), 11, 15, 18, 23,

55
John, Captain 56
John, Jr. 5
John, Sr. 20
Spencer A. 28
Thomas 5, 41
William 5, 11
Mount, Ezekiel 58
Moxley, Daniel 29
Joseph 41
Margaret 41
Samuel 41
William 41
Muir, Cato 15
George 15
James 15
Jeremiah 15
John 15
Phebe 15
Robert 9, 15
Samuel 15
Muirhead, Andrew 23, 24 (2)
William 23 (2), 24
Mull, David 45
George 45
Madlain 45
Margaret 45
Rachel 45
Munday, Aaron 58
Munroe, Spencer 58
Murphy, Ann 8
Martha 12
Michael 36
Murray, James 55
Samuel 18, 27, 29, 40
Musgrove, William 23, 25, 27 (2),
45
Myers, Andrew 32
Benj. 54
Christo. 54
Christopher 52
Elijah 37
George E. 64
George W. 64 (2)
Isaiah 37
Jacob 45
Jonathan 35, 37
Josiah 37
Mary 20, 37
Mary V. 64
Sarah E. 64
William 54

--- N ---

N..., Mary 42
Nance, Agnes 52
Samuel 52
Nandeern, Barnard 29
Nane, James 40
Naomi, Elizabeth 39
Neal, --- 55
Christopher 22
Penny 41
Roaham (Rodham) 41
Neale, Kitty 28
Richard 36
Robert 18
Thomas 19
Near, John 57
Neice, Devault 54
Neilson, William 31
Nelson, Israel 48
William 30
Neptune, John 18
Ruth 18

Sarah 18
Netson, Israel 48
Nevill, Lewis 12
Newell, John 33
    Margaret 33
    Rachel 33
    Sarah 33
    Seble 33
    Susan 33
    William 33
Newman, Elizabeth 32, 39
    George 39
    Joseph 39
    Richard 39
    Thomas 32
Newton, Charles A. 64 (2)
    Francis 64
    Sarah Wallace Hunter 64
Nichols, Isaac 18
    Rebecca 18
Nickland, John 47
Nicklin, Elizabeth 49
    John 50
Nickolls, Ann 38
    George 48
    Henry 44
    Isaac 37, 44, 58
    James 32
    Nathan 48
    Susannah 44
Nickols, Anne 37
    Charity 38
    George 38
    Henry 43, 54
    Isaac 55
    Isiah 38
    James 37, 38
    Mary 38
    Nathan 38 (2)
    Rebekka 38
    Solomon 38
    Thomas 55
Niles, Josias, Ensign 56
    Josias, 1st Lt. 56
Nines, Ann 3
Nixon, Elener 41
    Eliza 64
    Florence 64
    George 6, 39 (2), 54, 59
    J.L. 64
    James 22
    Joel 64 (2)
    Joel Lewis 59
    Jonathan 39
    Joseph Westwood 64
    L.B., Rev. 64
    Levi 64 (2)
    Margaret 64
    Mary Jane 59, 64
    Timothy 42
Noddy, William 55
Noland, Awbrey 45
    Catherine 61
    Eneas 31
    Nancy 31
    P. (Peter) 58
    Peter 55
    Philip 22, 31, 45, 55, 58
    Philip Nelson 31
    Sall 31
    Sarah 31
    Thomas 31, 45
Norman, John 58
Norton, Edward 1, 55
Norris, Ann 59
    Ignatus 60
    Mary 60

--- O ---

Oayter, John 54
Oden, Alexander 64
    Henry 64
    Thomas 54
Off, Nicholas 9
Offutt, William M. 43
Oldacre, Henry 33
Oliphant, Samuel, Ensign 56
Oliver, Peter 7
Omehundro, Ann 3
O'Neal, Ferdinand 4
O'Neale, Ferdinand 27
Onsley, William 1
Oram, Henry 57
Orange, James 64
    Susannah 64
Orr, Jno. 54
    John 10, 13, 16, 19, 34
Osborn, E. 64
    Emily 64
    Flavius 64
    J. 64
    Joab 64 (2)
    Michael 29
    William 40
Osborne, Abner 31, 32, 35, 37,
      38, 50
    John 55
    Lydia 35
    Mary 35
    Nicholas 11, 35, 46, 55
    Richard 54
    William 31, 38
Osbourne, John 33
    Richard 33
    Samuel 33
    Sarah 33
    William 30, 33
Osburn, Flavius 64
    Hannah 16
    Richard 16
Ouldaker, Abner 32
    Eleanor 32
    Enor 32
    Henry 32
    Isaac 32
    John 32
    William 32
Ousley, William, 1st Lt. 56
Overfelt, Benjamin 14
Overfield, Elizabeth 50
    Hutson 50
    Martin 50
    Nancy 50
    Peter 54
    Susannah 16
Owen, James 49
    John 2
Owens, James 49
    Mary 13
    William 55
Owsley, John 55
    Pine 55
    Thomas 21, 55
    William 55
Oxley, Ann 14
    Brittain 14
    Everest 23
    Hannah 17
    Henning (Hennell) 14
    Henry 9, 14, 17
    Jenkin 51
    Jeremiah 17
    Jesse 14, 17
    Joel 17

John 17 (2)
Mary 17
Rachel 14, 17, 23, 46

--- P ---

Padgit, Francis 54
Paget, Francis 1
Pagit, Amy 46
    Frances 46
    Francis 46, 54
    Reuben 46
    Ruth 46
    Timothy 46, 48
Palmer, Abel 12, 39
    David 12
    Elizabeth 12, 39
    John 12
    Jonathan 12
    Priscilla 12
    Samuel 12
Pancoast, Israel 47
    Jane A. 64
    John 44
    Joseph 64 (2)
    Sarah 37
Parker, Eliza 49
Parrott, John 43, 44
Patten, Elizabeth 14
    H.J. 16, 18
    Henry 18
Patterson, Fleming 7
    Janney 19
    Margaret 52
    Neil 6
    Samuel 8
Paul, James 15
Paxten, Sarah 12
Payne, Abigail 30
    Anne 40
    Benjamin 37
    George 51
    Henry, 1st Lt. 56
    Sanford 4, 30
Peacock, Henry 64
    Mary 64
Peake, John 6, 15, 21, 25
Peckner, Peter 29
Peers, A...n 60
Perfect, Eramus 51
    Robert 38, 51
Perfects, Catherine 40
    Christopher 40
    Elizabeth 40
    James 40
    Robert 40
Perrel, Charity 8
Perry, Elizabeth 11
Person, Samuel 6
Peters, John 58
Pettet, Isaac 7
    John 7
    Margaret 7
Pew, Samuel 23
    Sarah 54
Peyton, Ann 7, 13, 19
    Chandler 45
    Craven 3, 7, 13, 19, 33, 55
    Frances 13
    Francis 7, 14, 19, 36, 55
    Margaret 7, 13, 19
    Valentine 13, 19, 35
    William 7, 13, 19
Philips, Benjamin 38
    Charity 38
    Edmund 3

James 55
Nancy 38
Sarah 38
Thomas 48
Phillen, Andrew 54
Phillips, Benjamin 32
    Catherine 5
    David 42
    Edmund 3
    Hannah 14
    Hester 32
    Israel 32
    Jeanna 5
    Jenkin 15
    Jenkind 5
    Jenkins 5, 14, 32
    John 5
    Mary 5 (2)
    Milford 5
    Nancy 32
    Nicholas 9
    Samuel 32
    Sarah 32
    Thomas 5 (2), 7, 32
    Thomas, Sr. 5
    Thos. 54
Pickett, William 7
Pierce, Elsie 14
    John 26
Pierpoint, Esther 37
Pierpont, Obed 52
Piggott, Samuel 54
Pike, Jonathan 34, 38
Pinkstone, Shadrack 57
Pinquite, Esther 52, 54
    Jain 52
    John 52
Pitts, Ezekiel 4
    Martha 4
Pitzer, Harman 27
Plackney, Sarah 1
Pleasants, Bentley 64
    Robert 64
    Sallie 64
Poling, Martin 44
    Samuel 44
Ponner, Jonathan 54
Pool, Ann 11, 39
    Benjamin 11, 39
    Daniel 27
    Dorothy 27
    Elizabeth 11, 27, 39
    Frances 27
    Hannah 11, 39
    Israel 39
    Joseph 11, 39
    Martha 11, 39
    Mary 39
    Rebecca 11
    Rebekah 39
    Sarah 11, 39
    Thomas 27
Poole, Benjamin 21, 55
    Jane 43
    Thomas 28
Pophin, Catherine 16
Popkins, John 35
Porter, Daniel 8
    Edward 3, 8
    Elias 8
    John Brinkley 8
    Mary 3, 8
    Mary M. 13
    William 8
Poston, Elijah 14
    Francis 14
    Samuel 14
    Sarah 14

Potten, H. J. 16
Potter, Ebenezer 60
    Elizabeth 60
    John 1
Potts, Ann 5
    David 5, 6 (3), 55
    David, Sr. 19
    Edward 6
    Elizabeth 6, 29, 35
    Ezekiel 19, 30, 35
    Hannah 6
    Jonas 1, 4, 5 (3), 6, 55
    Jonathan 5, 6, 55
    Mary 4, 6
    Nathan 29, 30, 33
    Rachel 6
    Samuel 4, 5, 6 (2), 54, 55
    Susannah 6
Poultney, Anthony 1
    Eleanor 1
    Jno. 58
    John 1 (2)
    Mary 1
    Sarah 1
Poulton, John 38
    Martha 38
Powell, Ann 38
    Burr 45
    Cordelia 64
    Edward B. 64
    Edward Burr 64
    Elizabeth Burr 64
    Elisha 48
    Hugh L. 64
    Hugh Lee 64
    John 48
    Leven 7, 8, 14, 15, 45 (2), 46,
      52, 57
    Lewellyn 64
    Lewis 21
    Mary 48
    Mary Susan 64
    Mary Lowden 64
    Robert 48
    Sarah 48, 61
    William 30, 38, 48
Power, Joseph 45
    Sarah 45
    Walter 45
Powers, Joseph 28
Preston, John 36
Price, Jonathan 13, 15, 23
    Oliver 16
    Sarah 15
    Susannah 39
    Thomas 39
Priest, Eleanor 16, 18
    Samuel 42
    William 16
Prudane, Jeremiah 41
Pryledieu, Margaret 33
Pugh, Samuel 30
Pullen, Charles 25, 54
Purdain, Benjamin 45
Purdin, Benjamin 22
Purdon, Benjamin 32
Purdum, Benjamin 46
Purdune, Jeremiah 45
Pursel, Sarah 33
Pursley, Benjamin 16
    Catherine 16
    Christiana 16
    Daniel 16
    Deborah 16
    Elizabeth 16
    Henry 16
    John 16
    Larrance 16

    Mary 16
    Samuel 16
    Thomas 16, 21
    William 16
Pyatt, Mary 49
Pyburn, Joshua 58
Pyley, Joseph Willis 60
Pyott, Amos 35
    John 35

--- Q ---

Queen, Jonah 41
Quick, Casper 13
    John 57

--- R ---

Radcliff, Edward 37
Radcliffe, John 2
    Susan 2
Ralls, George 54
Ramey, Benjamin 24, 54
    Jacob 34
    John, Sr. 34
Ratcliff, Edward 37
Rattekin, James 17
Ray, William 26
Rayley, Nathan 24
Reach, Richard 54
Read, Andrew 2
    Ann 3
    Barbara 2
    Elizabeth 2
    Frances 2
    Jacob 8
    John 2
    Joseph 2, 55
    Lettice 2
    Reuben 2
    Ruth 3
    Thaddeus 2
    William 2
Reade, John 32
    Reuben 32
    William 32
Reamy, Sanford 34
Record, Joseph 28
Rector, Harry 31
Redman, Andrew 50
    John 45, 50
    Mary 50
Redmand, George 4
Redmond, Andrew 3
    Ann 3
    Elizabeth 3
    John 3, 54
    Margaret 3
    Sarah 3
    William 3
Reed, A... G. 50
    Andrew 38, 54
    Cornelius 38
    Eleanor 42
    Elizabeth 38
    Eunus (Eunice) 38
    Frances 61
    Jacob 20, 21, 58
    Jacob, Major 56
    John Grigsby 50
    Jonathan 7, 38
    Lewis Grigsby 50
    Ludwell Grigsby 50
    Mary 50

Naomi 38
Nathaniel Grigsby 50
Osse 36
R. 47
Stephen 38
Susannah 38
William 47
Reeder, Daniel 8
David 8
Elener 8
Elijah 8
Elizabeth 8, 57
Jacob 8
Joseph 8
Mary 8
Shadrack 57
Stephen 8
William 8
Rees, Edward 38
Reid, Frances 61
Jacob 29
Rebecca 29
Reigor, John 18
Remey, Benjamin Talbot 30
Betty 40
Elijah 30
Elizabeth 30
Henry 30
Jacob 30, 34, 40, 55
Jacob, Jr. 21
Jacob, Sr. 21
John, Sr. 34
Rebecca 30
Sanford 34
William 3
Repess, Thomas 26
Thomas, Captain 56
Thomas, Lt. Col. 56
Thomas, Major 56
Respess, Thomas 18
Retan, E. 59
Ellen 59
Reynolds, Rachel 8
Rhoades, Moses 55
Rhodes, Abigail 7
Ann 7
Elizabeth 7
George 51
Hannah 7
Jacob 26, 57
John 7
Joseph 29
Martha 53
Mary 7, 57
Moses 5, 7
Thomas 7
William 7, 51
Rice, David 60
Elizabeth 60
Hannah 57
James 57
Jesse 60
Joab 20
Thirza 60
Rich, Samuel 14, 16, 24
Richards, Ann 57
Esther 53
Lydia 30
Thomas 57
William 30
Richardson, James 17, 23
John 17
Mary 30
Richie, Frantz 10
Riely, Robert 15
Riena, Dinah 18
Right, William 50
Rightmire, Benjamin 36

Riley, Robert 15
Rine, George 18
Ringo, Cornelius 18
Margaret 18
Rinker, Edward 30, 57
Sarah 30
Ritchardson, Joseph 45
Ritchey, Isaac 52
Ritchie, John 28
Rittenhouse, Benjamin Franklin,
Major 64
Roach, Edmund 54
Hannah 12
James 12
Richard 38, 55
Robert, Richard, Gent. 58 (2)
Roberts, Ann 2
Eleanor 18
Jane 18
Jean 16
John 2
Joseph 2
Mary 2
Owen 6 (3), 8, 12, 16
Richard 2, 55
Susanah 2
William 2, 16, 42
Robertson, Henry 7
Jenny 7
Susannah 39
William 39
Robeson, Ann 8
Sylvana 8
Robinett, Allen 6
Robison, Elizabeth 19
John 19
Nancy 19
Sarah 19
Roger, Mary 64
Rogers, Alec 64
Richard 12
Roler, John 54
Rolow, Ellen 60
Ezra 60
Romine, Abigail 35
John 35
Peter 14, 35
Ruth 33
Sarah 35
Rooney, M. 41
Roper, Elizabeth 40, 54
Joseph 28
Nancy 40
Thomas 27
Rose, Anna 60
George, Col. 60
James 39
John, Captain 60
Ross, William 2 (2), 13
Roxbury, M. W. 64
Roy, William 26
Rozel, Stephen 6
Rozell, Anthony 9
Nancy 41
Phebe 41
Sally 41
Sarah 9, 41
Stephen 15, 22
Rozzell, Stephens 41
Rush, Vylinda H. 64
Russell, A. 42
Albert 42, 47
Ann 47
Anthony 3, 8, 16, 17, 55
Anthony, Col. 16
Benjamin 60
Elizabeth 45
Frances 18

Francis 17
Francis, Capt. 20
John 57
Mary McDowell 45
Melea 42
Milly 17
Penelope 17
Robert 45, 52
Robert, 2nd Lt. 56
Samuel 55, 57
Sarah 57
Thomas, Col. 24
William 9
Rust, George, 2nd Lt. 56
William 37
Ryon, John Bowan 43

--- S ---

Said, John 15
Sainclare, Margaret 3
Saintclare, Margaret 3
Sambrey, --- 55
Samuel, Isaac 6
Samuels, Shadrack 30
Sanders, --- 62 (3)
Aaron 15, 49, 52
Barbara 15
Barbary 49
Benjamin 6
Betheny 49
Beverly 64
Cyrus 15
Elizabeth 6, 49
Gunnell 15
Gunnell, Lt. 56
Henry 15
James 15, 17, 21, 24, 27, 49
James, Sr. 26
John 15, 49
John, Ensign 56
Mary 49
Moses 15
Nancy 49
Patience 49
Philip 6
Polly 48
Pressley 15, 49
Sarah 15, 49
Thomas 15
William 6, 25
Wilson 64
Sands, Benjamin 12, 18
Edmund 12, 22
Edward 55
Gideon 12
Isaac 12, 54
Israel 12
Joseph 12
Sarah 12
Sanford, Daniel 42
Elizabeth 42
Henry 42
John 42
Rebecca 42
Santeclares, John 3
Margaret 3
Saunders, James 14
Scatterday, Esther 6
George 6
John 6
Schooley, Ann 34
Dorothy 34
Hannah 44
Jesse 34
John 20, 34

Reuben 32
Thomas 3, 11
Thomas Ballard 11
Sorrill, Reuben 32
Sothard, Larance 4
Sother, William 4
Sotherd, Sarah 4
Sothern, Christiana 65 (3)
William 65 (3)
Southard, William 45
Spence, John 11
Spencer, America 64, 65
James 57
John 4
Nathan 19
Spindle, Priscilla 65
R.L. 65
Spitfathen, Benjamin 57
Spitz, Benjamin 57
Spoon, Elizabeth 39
Spurr, Frances 35
James 1
Judath 1
Richard 1, 2, 11, 25, 34
Squires, Ann 17, 18
Elizabeth 37
Sally 17
Thomas 17, 23
Stanhope, William 15, 19, 20, 22,
24, 48, 49
Stapleton, Thomas 21
Stark, Elizabeth 10
John 10
Nancy 10
Susan 10
William 2 (2), 10, 22
Starkhart, George 29
Statler, Abraham 24
Statner, Jacob 28
Steadman, John W. 65
Lillian 65
Steer, Benjamin 33
Isaac 51
John 51
Joseph 51
Steere, Amos 54
Ann 54
James 1, 2
John 21, 54
Stephen, Martin 37
Stephens, Ann 30
Benjamin 51
Cleo 11
Edward 11
Eleanor 30, 32, 38 (2)
Elizabeth 30
Ezekiel 54
George 51
Giles 11, 21
Henry 51
Hezekiah 51
James 11, 51
John 65
John A. 65
Joseph 4, 30, 38 (2)
Richard 32, 38
Robert 32, 38
Roxanna 65
Thomas 11
William 51
Zachariah 51
Sterrett, Samuel 60
Stevens, Alice 17
H. 54
Hannah 11, 17, 46, 51
James 17, 54
Robert 12
Stewart, Daniel 54

H. 44
Stocks, John 65
Stoker, Michael 58
Stokes, John 57
Stone, Henry 24
Jane 51
Rachel 49
Samuel 55
Thomas 55
Stoneberger, John 58
Stowell, Thomas 22
Street, Martin 27
Stroud, Samuel 54
Stroupe, Mary Ann 29
Milcher 29
Strowd, Ann 4
George 4
James 4
Samuel 4
Susan 4
Stukesberry, Robert 58
Robert, Sr. 58
Stump, C. 49
Elizabeth 1
Jacob 49
Jane 1
Peter 50
Thomas 1, 55
Sulton, Mary 9
Summers, Francis 54
George 30, 34, 41
George, Captain 56
Grant, Sr. 55
Margaret 41
Polly 41
Sutherland, Alexander 58
Sutton, Mary 9
Swain, Joseph 7
Swart, Adrian 36, 54
Elizabeth 52
John 52, 54
Swick, Anthony 14
Swindler, Henry 43
Swink, Adam 19
Jane 19
John 20
Rachel 19

--- T ---

Talbert, Ann 18
Anne 18
Benjamin 18
Frances 18
Henry 24
John 18
William 18
Talbot, Barbara 30
Benjamin 30
Hannah Neale 30
Henry 30
Talbott, Ann 52
D. 43
Elisha 52
Elizabeth 52
Hannah 38
Henry 27
Jesse 52
John 52
Joseph 52, 54
Mary 52
Rebekah 52
Samuel 52
Sarah 52
Susannah 52
Talbut, Anna 5

Talbutt, Hannah 30
Tallbott, Joseph 54
Tanny, Joseph 12
Tavenor, George 12
Taverner, George 20
Susannah 35
Tawner, John 54
Tayloe, John 33
Taylor, Ambrose 52
Ann 49
Bernard 52 (2)
Craven 37
Cybitha 37
Elizabeth 37
Evan 54
George 26, 37
Handley 37
Henry 9, 21, 49
Henry, Sr. 9
Jack T. 37
James 50
Jesse 32 49
John 6 (2), 9
John, 1st Lt. 56
Jonathan 52
Joseph 49
Joshua 9
Mary 49
Patty 28
Rachel 49
Sarah 49
Stacy 44, 50, 53
Stephen 37
Susannah 9
Thomas 45, 49
Timothy 48
Walter 9
William 18, 21, 37, 52
William, Major 56
Tebbs, --- 62 (2)
A.S. 60 (2)
Ann Cleveland 65
Charles 65
Fanny 65
H.S. 62
J.E. 60 (2)
Mary 60, 65
S.J. 62
W. W., Capt. 65
William 60
William, Capt. 65
Tebit, Hannah 41
John 41
Telliafero, John 31
Tennant, Eugenia 62
Tethern, Cathy 41
Thacker, John 26
Richard 26
Thatcher, John 38
Joseph 54
Richard 38, 43 (2)
Thomas, Amy 5
Anne 10
Benjamin 43
Catherine 42, 44
David 1, 35, 40, 48
Dorothy 39
Elizabeth 1
Emmett 11
Enoch, 2nd Lt. 56
Evan 1, 8
George 48, 51
Griffith 54
Hannah 29, 35
Humphrey 9
James 1, 60 (2)
John 13, 19, 33, 42, 44
Joseph 6, 29, 42

West, Ann 3, 7
   Anna Brown 33
   C. 36
   Cato 3, 7
   Charles 3, 7, 13, 33
   Elizabeth 7, 13, 33
   George 6, 58
   George, Captain 56
   George, Colonel 56
   George, Lt. Col. 56
   John 7, 47, 49, 58
   Margaret 13
   Mary 7
   Thomas 7, 13, 23
   W. 5
   William 3, 7
   William, Capt. 56
   William, Jr. 3
Westwood, George H. 65
   W. 65
Whaley, Ann 30
   Barbara 30, 34
   Ben 30
   Elijah 30
   Elizabeth 30
   Gilson 34
   Henry 30
   James 23, 25, 30, 31, 36, 54
   James, 2nd Lt. 56
   John 34
   Penelope 30, 38
   Rebecca 30
   William 30, 34 (2), 38
Whealer, Mary 37
Wheeler, Ignatus 31
Wherry, --- 60
   Elizabeth 60
   Mary E. 60
   Silas 60
Whitacre, Benjamin 31
   Caleb 31, 39
   Edward 48
   Elizabeth 31
   Enuck 31
   George 31
   John 44
   Joseph 31
   Joshua 31
   Martha 31, 48
   Neomy 31
   Robert 31
   Ruth 31
White, Ann 39
   Benjamin 39
   Daniel 39
   E.V., Col. 65 (2)
   James 51, 54
   Joel, Ensign 56
   Joel, 2nd Lt. 56
   John 24
   Joseph 39
   Josiah 16 (2), 24
   Mary Elizabeth 65 (4)
   Mathew 26
   Melvin 65
   Rebekah 39
   Richard 39, 65
   Robert 52
   Rosa Lee 65
   Samuel 39
   Stephen 65
   William 39
Whitely, William 6, 26
Whitmore, Michael 54
Wigginton, Benjamin 15, 58
   Eleanor 15
   Elinor 15

   Elizabeth 15
   Henry 15
   James 39
   Roger 15
   Roger, Sr. 15
   Spencer 17
   William 15, 17
Wigington, Benjamin 4
   James 4
   John 4
   Sarah 4
   Robert 25
   Roger 24, 25
Wihen, William 9
Wilcox, Eleanor 57
Wilcoxen, Agnes 4
   Elizabeth 4
   John 4
   Mary 4
Wildman, Abraham 39
   Jacob 2, 3
   Joseph, 2nd Lt. 56
   Letitia 39
   Robert 65
   William 2
Wildmore, Joseph 24
Wilkes, Francis 56
   John 56
Wilkins, James 65
Wilkinson, Evan 23
   Joseph 54
Wilks, Samuel 12, 38
William, Original 2
Williams, Abner 33
   Agatha 35
   America Spencer 65
   Ann 45
   David 11
   Elijah 14
   Elizabeth 33
   Enos 49
   Hannah 33
   Henry 33
   J. 52
   James 49, 60, 65 (2)
   Jenkins 35, 49
   John 33, 47, 65 (2)
   Joseph 49
   Joshua 35
   Margaret 49
   Mary 54
   Notley 9
   Pleasants H. 65
   Rehoboth 33
   Richard 8, 21, 49
   Susannah 47
   Thomas 11
   Uncie 33
   Ureah 35
   Walker 56
   Will 56
   William 9, 10, 33
Williamson, Nancy 46
Willoughby, Mary 65
Willson, Henry Lawerence 34
   John 34
   John Jeff 34
   Kezia 34
   Maria 34
   Mary 34
Wils, Samuel 12
Wilson, ---, Mr. 7
   Alex 41
   Caroline 62
   Elener 41
   Elizabeth 41

   James 19, 41
   John 36
   Mary 19
   Russell 3
Wincill, Jacob 41
Wingarden, Harbard 24
Wingardner, Harbard 17
   Henry 17
Winser, John 4
Winsor, Thomas 56
   William 56
Winzel, Adam 10
   Elizabeth 10
Wirts, Anna Mary 51
   Catherine 51
   Christina 51
   Jacob 51
   John 51
   Michael 51
   Peter 51 (2)
   William 51
Wiseheart, Henry 13, 56
Wohund, Elizabeth 46
Wolf, John 29
Wood, Lashley 17
   Mary 19
   Milly 19
   Samuel 24
Woodward, Annie 65
   Jesse 11
   John 65
   Newton 65
   Prudence 11, 45
Wooland, William 24
Woolard, William 17
Wornell, James 58
   Thomas 24
Wrenn, Susanah 24
Wright, Anthony 22
   Margaret 45
   Martha 29, 35
   Mary 1
   Robert 25, 27, 45
   William 29, 50
Wyatt, Abner 10
   Edward 10
   John 10
   Margaret 10
   Reuben 10
   Ruth 10
   Thomas 10, 21
Wychoff, Nicholas 12
Wyman, Robert 52
Wynkoor, Linnie A. 65
Wynn, Robert 45

--- W ---

Yates, Alice 2
   Benjamin 2
   Hannah 2
   Isaac 2
   Jane 2
   Joseph 2 (2)
   Providence 2
   Robert 2
   Samuel 26
   William 2
Yeates, Benjamin 15
   George 15
   Johannah 15
   Joshua 15
   Samuel 15
Youts, John 22